What was the Enlightenment? Was it a unified body of thought generated by an established canon of 'great thinkers', or were there many areas of contradiction and divergence? How far-reaching were its critiques intended to be? Was it a revolutionary body of thought, or was it merely a catalyst for the revolutionary age which followed? Did it mean the same for men and for women, for rich and poor, or for European and non-European?

In this important new textbook Dorinda Outram addresses these, and other questions about the 'Enlightenment'. She sets the major debates of the period against the broader social changes such as the onset of industrialisation in Western Europe, the establishment of new colonial empires, and the exploration of hitherto unmapped portions of the world's surface. This unique and accessible synthesis of scholarship will be invaluable to any student of eighteenth-century history.

New approaches to European history

The Enlightenment

NEW APPROACHES TO EUROPEAN HISTORY

Series editors
WILLIAM BEIK *Emory University*
T. C. W. BLANNING *Sidney Sussex College, Cambridge*
R. W. SCRIBNER *Clare College, Cambridge*

New Approaches to European History is an important new textbook initiative, intended to provide concise but authoritative surveys of major themes and problems in European history since the Renaissance. Written at a level and length accessible to advanced school students and undergraduates, each book in the series will address topics or themes that students of European history encounter daily: the series will embrace both some of the more 'traditional' subjects of study, and those cultural and social issues to which increasing numbers of school and college courses are devoted. A particular effort will be made to consider the wider international implications of the subject under scrutiny.

To aid the student reader scholarly apparatus and annotation will be light, but each work will have full supplementary bibliographies and notes for further reading: where appropriate chronologies, maps, diagrams, and other illustrative material will be provided.

The Enlightenment

Dorinda Outram

University College, Cork

CAMBRIDGE
UNIVERSITY PRESS

Published by the Press Syndicate of the University of Cambridge
The Pitt Building, Trumpington Street, Cambridge CB2 1RP
40 West 20th Street, New York, NY 10011-4211, USA
10 Stamford Road, Oakleigh, Melbourne 3166, Australia

First published 1995
Reprinted 1996, 1997, 1998

Printed in Great Britain at the University Press, Cambridge

A catalogue record for this book is available from the British Library

Library of Congress cataloguing in publication data

Outram, Dorinda.
The Enlightenment / Dorinda Outram.
  p.   cm. – (New approaches to European history ; 6)
Includes bibliographical references and index.
ISBN 0 521 41522 5. – ISBN 0 521 42534 4 (pbk.)
1. Enlightenment.   2. Europe–Intellectual life–18th century.
I. Title.   II. Series.
B802.098   1995
001.1′094′09033–dc20   94-35014 CIP

ISBN 0 521 41522 5 hardback
ISBN 0 521 42534 4 paperback

SE

Dedication
To my past pupils in History Option HI222, *The Enlightenment*, who made me think harder; and for Veronica Fraser who made this book possible.

Contents

Illustrations

Chronology

1686	German Pietist August Francke (1663–1727) opens Bible study at Leipzig; Charles Duke of Lorraine, takes Buda from the Turks
1687	Isaac Newton, *Philosophiae Naturalis Principia Mathematica*
1688	William of Orange ousts James II as King of England
1689	John Locke, *Letters on Toleration*
1690	John Locke, *An Essay Concerning Human Understanding*
1691	New East India Company formed in London
1693	John Locke, *Thoughts Concerning Education*
1694	Founding of Bank of England. Birth of Voltaire
1695	John Locke, *The Reasonableness of Christianity*
1697	Peter the Great travels to Prussia, Holland, England and Vienna to study European technology and thought
1702	Asiento Guinea Company founded for slave trade between Africa and America
1704	Isaac Newton, *Optics*
1707	Political and legal union between England and Scotland. Linnaeus born
1709	First Copyright Act in Britain
1713	Abbé de St Pierre, *Projet pour la paix perpétuelle* Peace of Utrecht closes war of Spanish Succession
1715	Louis XIV of France dies; succeeded by his great-grandson Louis XV, under Regency of the Duc d'Orléans
1716	First company of English actors appears in North America at Williamsburg, Virginia
1717	Innoculation against small pox introduced into England from Turkey by Lady Mary Wortley Montagu (1690–1762). First Freemasons' Lodge established in London
1718	Yale University founded at New Haven, Connecticut; New Orleans founded
1719	Daniel Defoe, *Robinson Crusoe*
1721	Montesquieu, *Lettres Persanes*; J.S. Bach, 'Brandenburg Concertos'. Regular postal service between London and New England
1722	Daniel Defoe, *Moll Flanders*
1723	Ludovico Antonio Muratori publishes *Rerum italicarum scrip-*

tores, 28 vols. of medieval documents. End of Regency in France. Bach, 'St John Passion'

1724   Professorships of modern history founded at Oxford and Cambridge. Paris Bourse (Stock Exchange) opens

1725   Foundation of Petersburg Academy of Sciences; of Prague Opera House. Vico, *Principles of a New Science*

1726   Jonathan Swift, *Gulliver's Travels*. Voltaire arrives in England

1727   American Philosophical Society founded in Philadelphia. Isaac Newton died

1728   Ephraim Chambers (ed.), *Cyclopaedia or An Universal Dictionary of Arts and Sciences*

1729   J.S. Bach, 'St Matthew Passion', Newton's *Principia* translated into English

1730   John and Charles Wesley found Methodism at Oxford

1731   Abbé Prévost, *Manon Lescaut*; Voltaire, *History of Charles XII*. Franklin founds subscription library at Philadelphia

1732   Covent Garden Opera House founded in London

1733   War of the Polish Succession opens. Alexander Pope, *Essay on Man*

1734   University of Göttingen founded; Koran translated into English by George Sale

1735   Francesco Algorotti, *Il newtonismo per le Dame*; Carl Linnaeus, *Systema Naturae*

1738   Papal Bull *In eminenti* condemns Freemasonry. Excavations begin at Herculaneum. Voltaire, *Eléments de la philosophie de Newton*

1739   David Hume, *A Treatise of Human Nature*

1740   Frederick II becomes King of Prussia and founds Berlin Academy of Sciences. Maria Theresa becomes Empress of Austria. Frederick seizes Silesia, opening war of the Austrian succession. Samuel Richardson, *Pamela*. George Anson (1697–1762) begins circumnavigation of globe

1741   Handel composes 'The Messiah'

1746   Condillac, *Essai sur l'origine des connaissances humaines*

1747   La Mettrie, *L'homme machine*

1748   End of War of Austrian Succession; Marie-Thérèse Geoffrin opens *salon*; Samuel Richardson, *Clarissa*; David Hume, *Philosophical Essay Concerning Human Understanding*; Montesquieu, *De l'esprit des lois*

1750   Rousseau, *Discours sur les sciences et les arts*; Jewish sect of Hassidism founded

1751   First volume of Diderot and d'Alembert's *Encyclopédie*; David

Hume, *Enquiry Concerning the Principles of Morals*; Voltaire, *Le Siècle de Louis XIV*; Pope Benedict XIV condemns Freemasonry

1752   First condemnation of the *Encyclopédie*

1754   David Hume, *History of Great Britain*; Diderot, *Pensées sur l'Interprétation de la Nature*; Rousseau, *L'inégalité parmi les hommes: discours*

1755   Earthquake in Lisbon; Samuel Johnson, *Dictionary of the English Language*

1756   Beginning of Seven Years' War

1758   Claude Adrien Helvétius, *De L'Esprit*; Rousseau, *Lettre à d'Alembert sur les spectacles*; Quesnay, *Tableau Economique*

1759   Second condemnation of the *Encyclopédie*; Jesuits expelled from Portugal; Voltaire, *Candide*; Charles III succeeds as King of Spain; Samuel Johnson, *Rasselas*; Adam Smith, *Theory of Moral Sentiments*; British Museum open in London, at Montague House; Wolfe takes Quebec from the French

1760   George III becomes king in Great Britain.

1761   Rousseau, *La Nouvelle Héloïse*

1762   Catherine II becomes Empress of Russia; Diderot, *Le Neveu de Rameau*; Rousseau, *Du Contrat Social*, *Emile*; Calas trial

1763   Peace of Paris ends Seven Years' War. Voltaire, *Treatise on Toleration*

1764   Jesuits suppressed in France. Salons founded in Paris by Mme. Necker and Julie de Lespinasse. Cesare Becarria, *Dei Delitti e dei Pene*; Voltaire, *Philosophical Dictionary*; J.J. Wincklemann, *History of Ancient Art*

1765   Joseph II becomes co-regent with his mother Maria Theresa; Turgot, *Réflexions sur la formation et la distribution des richesses*

1766   Adam Ferguson, *Essay on the History of Civil Society*; Bougainville begins voyage to Pacific

1767   Rousseau in England. Jesuits expelled from Spain and Naples. Laurence Sterne completes *Tristram Shandy*. Joseph Priestley, *The History and Present State of Electricity*

1768   Purchase of Corsica by France from Genoa; Quesnay, *Physiocratie*. James Cook's first voyage to the Pacific

1769   William Robertson (1721–93), *History of Charles V*; Diderot writes *Le Rêve d'Alembert*

1770   Court Doctor von Struensee becomes Chief Minister in Denmark. Cook lands at Botany Bay, Australia. Raynal, *Histoire . . . des Deux Indes*; D'Holbach, *Système de la Nature*

1771   French *Parlements* exiled. Rising tension between them and monarchy. First edition of *Encyclopedia Britannica*. William Robertson, *History of America*: Arkwright produces first spinning mill; Luigi Galvani discovers electrical nature of nervous impulses; Lavoisier establishes composition of air

1772   Fall of Danish reformer Struensee; First partition of Poland; James Cook's second circumnavigation begins

1773   Boston Tea Party. Pope Clement XIV dissolves Jesuit order

1774   Louis XV of France dies, succeeded by Louis XVI. Goethe, *The Sorrows of Werther*. Turgot becomes minister

1775   American War of Independence begins. Peasant revolt in Bohemia against serfdom; Beaumarchais, *The Barber of Seville*; 'Guerre des farines' in Paris and Northern France

1776   Declaration of Independence by American rebels, mainly drafted by Thomas Jefferson. Turgot forced out of government; Edward Gibbon, *Decline and Fall of the Roman Empire* (-1788); Adam Smith, *An Inquiry into the Nature and Causes of the Wealth of Nations*. James Cook begins third voyage into the Pacific

1778   James Cook discovers Hawaii. Deaths of Voltaire and Rousseau; Buffon, *Les époques de la Nature*

1779   James Cook murdered. Serfdom suppressed in France and its colonies. David Hume, *Dialogues of Natural Religion* (posthumous publication)

1780   Empress Maria Theresa dies; Joseph II succeeds as sole ruler. Filangieri, *Science of Legislation*. Abolition of judicial torture in France

1781   Kant, *Critique of Pure Reason*; Rousseau, *Confessions*, published; Mendelssohn, *On the Civil Amelioration of the Condition of the Jews*

1782   Laclos, *Les Liaisons dangéreuses*

1783   American colonies win independence from Britain. Mendelssohn, *Jerusalem*, plea for religious toleration

1784   Bengal Asiatic Society founded by William Jones

1785   William Paley, *Principles of Moral and Political Philosophy*

1786   Death of Frederick II. Mozart, *Marriage of Figaro*

1787   Rising political tension in France. Meeting of the first Assembly of Notables. Lavoisier reforms chemical language with *Méthode de nomenclature chimique*. Mozart, *Don Giovanni*

1788   Elections for the Estates-General in France. Kant, *Critique of Practical Reason*. Pierre Simon de la Place; *Laws of the Planetary System*

1789   Estates General meets (May). Mutiny on the *Bounty*

1790   Joseph II dies. Edmund Burke, *Reflections on the Revolution in France*
1791   Thomas Paine, *The Rights of Man*
1792   Mary Wollstonecraft, *Vindication of the Rights of Women*
        France at war with Austria and Prussia
1793   Second partition of Poland. Condorcet, *Esquisse d'un tableau historique des progrès de l'esprit humain*

I   What is Enlightenment?

The time will come when the sun will shine
only on free men who have no master but their reason.   (Condorcet)[1]

Debate over the meaning of 'Enlightenment' began in the eighteenth
century itself and has continued unabated until our own times. Even in
the eighteenth century, contemporaries were well aware that the spread of
words used in different linguistic areas to refer to 'Enlightenment' –
Aufklärung in German, *Lumières* in French, *Illuminismo* in Italian –
betrayed a fundamental diversity at the heart of 'the Enlightenment'.[2] It
was thus not surprising that in 1783, the influential Berlin newspaper, the
Berlinische Monatsschrift, asked for responses to the simple yet crucial
question of 'What is Enlightenment?'. The essays submitted to the paper
in response came from men as diverse as the dramatist Gothold Lessing
(1729–81), the Jewish philosopher Moses Mendelssohn (1729–86) and
the Prussian philosopher Immanuel Kant (1724–1804), as well as many
others. These essays can be read as a compendium of the diverse meanings
that by the end of the century had come to be attached to the term
'Enlightenment'.[3] For Mendelssohn, 'Enlightenment' was a difficult
term to define, because it referred to a *process*, far from complete in his
own day, of education for man, an education in the use of 'reason' – a key
word in 'Enlightenment' thinking. At the same time, Mendelssohn was
well aware that the unlimited development of 'reason' in individuals
might well conflict with their role as subjects and citizens. 'Reason', if
carried too far with unlimited questioning and redefinition, could dis-
solve social, religious and political order into chaos and leave men isolated

---

[1] Quoted in E. Cassirer, *Rousseau, Kant and Goethe* (New York, 1963)
[2] H. Stuke, 'Aufklärung', in O. Brunner, W. Conze and R. Kosselleck (eds.), *Geschichtliche Grundbegriffe, Historisches Lexikon zur politisch-sozialen Sprache in Deutschland* (Stutt-gart, 1972), I, 244; F. Venturi, 'Contributi ad un dizionario storico: 'Was ist *Aufklärung? Sapere aude*', *Rivista storica italiano*, 71 (1959), 112–43.
[3] N. Hinske (ed.), *Was ist Aufklärung? Beiträge aus der Berlinischen Monatsschrift*, 2nd edn (Darmstadt, 1977); E. Behr (ed.), *Was ist Aufklärung? Thesen und Definitionen* (Stuttgart, 1974). Jean Mondot (ed.), *Immanuel Kant, Qu'est-ce que les Lumières? Choix de textes (1780–1790)* (Paris, 1991).

in intellectual egoism. Nor was this a problem merely raised by theoreticians. Only a few years before, in 1780, that eminently practical ruler Frederick the Great of Prussia (1712–86), had directed the Berlin Academy of Sciences to offer a prize for the best essay responding to the question 'Is it expedient to deceive the people?'. That this became the most popular competition in the Academy's history and generated great public interest across Europe, reveals a widespread recognition, by the closing years of the eighteenth century, that *Aufklärung* was important – important enough to pose great potential problems for governments searching for a political relationship with the power of organised knowledge in society.[4] It was also a recognition of the difficulty and complexity of any answer to the issue.

These were themes which were also pursued in Immanuel Kant's contribution to the *Berlinische Monatsschrift*.[5] This brief article is probably one of the most quoted and least well-understood attempts to grapple with the meaning of 'Enlightenment'. Kant calls 'Enlightenment', in a much-quoted phrase, 'man's release from his self incurred immaturity', by the use of his own reason, undistorted by prejudice and without the guidance of others. '*Sapere aude*, have the courage to know: this is the motto of Enlightenment', writes Kant, also near the beginning of the essay. But other, far less quoted, parts of Kant's essay, present a much more complex picture of Enlightenment, for example, when he remarks: 'The public use of man's reason must always be free and it alone can bring about Enlightenment among men; the private use of reason may be quite often seriously restricted.' In the public sphere, subjects of a ruler have an actual duty to restrain the expression of wayward individual judgement in the interests of upholding the ruler's will and thus lessening the likelihood of the outbreak of chaos and insecurity. Kant poses, in different words, the same problem as Mendelssohn had done: What happens if men think without limits? Does such thought necessarily have a positive outcome? Kant makes clear his impatience with those of his contemporaries who saw their own time as one of unbounded progress towards the fulfillment of human potential, or of the achievement of 'rational' social and political arrangements. Like Mendelssohn, Kant was clear that 'Enlightenment' was a process, not a completed project; and a process, at that, fraught with dangers and problems. 'If it is now asked whether we live at present in an Enlightened age, the answer is: No, but we do live in an age of Enlightenment.'

---

[4] These essays are reprinted in W. Krauss (ed.), *Est-il utile de tromper le peuple? Ist der Volkbetrug von Nutzen? Concours de la classe de philosophie speculative de l'Académie des Sciences et de Belles Lettres de Berlin pour l'année 1780* (Berlin, 1966).

[5] H. Reiss (ed.), *Kant's Political Writings* (Cambridge, 1977), 54–60.

Even for Mendelssohn and Kant, therefore, Enlightenment was not an easy word to define. And for both men, Enlightenment seemed to present itself more as a series of processes and *problems* than as a list of intellectual projects susceptible to quick and definitive description. These are perceptions which will be incorporated into the framework of discussion in this book. Rather than attempting some neat definition of Enlightenment, which would always be open to challenge or qualification, it is more helpful to think of Enlightenment as a series of problems and debates, of 'flash-points', characteristic of the eighteenth century, or of 'pockets' where projects of intellectual expansion impacted upon and changed the nature of developments in society and government on a world-wide basis. Some of the most important of these problems have already been touched upon, in particular the contradiction between unrestricted inquiry and the need to assure stability in state and society.[6]

This way of looking at the Enlightenment as a series of debates, which necessarily took different shapes and forms in particular national and cultural contexts, is however, a relatively new one. Generally speaking, up until about twenty years ago, historians of this period usually thought of *the* Enlightenment, as a relatively unitary phenomenon in the history of ideas, ideas generated by an established canon of 'great thinkers', such as Charles-Louis Montesquieu (1689–1755), Denis Diderot (1713–84), or Kant. These thinkers shared the obvious characteristics of being white, male and drawn from western Europe. While acknowledging many differences of opinion on individual issues between the great thinkers, historians still tended usually to see their ideas, the ideas of *the* Enlightenment in the last analysis as relatively homogeneous. In this interpretation, Enlightenment was a desire for human affairs to be guided by rationality rather than by faith, superstition, or revelation; a belief in the power of human reason to change society and liberate the individual from the restraints of custom or arbitrary authority; all backed up by a world view increasingly validated by science rather than by religion or tradition. A landmark in this approach to the Enlightenment was Ernst Cassirer's *The Philosophy of the Enlightenment*, which defined the Enlightenment as a period bounded by the lives of two philosophers: Gottfried Wilhelm Leibniz (1646–1716) and Immanuel Kant (1724–1804).[7] In Cassirer's words, the Enlightenment was 'a value-system rooted in rationality', a definition of the past which must have possessed considerable attraction in the notoriously irrational 1930s in Europe. This line of interpretation of the Enlightenment saw it as an intellectual movement by great thinkers

---

[6] This is a problem which will be examined more closely in chapters 7 and 8.

[7] Ernst Cassirer, *The Philosophy of the Enlightenment* (Boston, 1964; originally published, 1932).

in Western Europe and displayed little interest in its social or political context, or in the impact of these ideas. This was a viewpoint which in many ways was developed and continued by the American historian Peter Gay, in his synthesis of Enlightenment thought which began to appear in 1966.[8] Individual volume titles (*The Rise of Modern Paganism* and *The Science of Freedom*), clearly indicate Gay's agenda in interpreting the Enlightenment. Like Cassirer, he defines the Enlightenment as a unity,[9] and defines its chronology in terms of the lives of great thinkers. For Gay, the first period or 'generation' of the Enlightenment was that of Voltaire (1694–1778) and Montesquieu (1689–1755), followed by the second, that of Denis Diderot (1713–84), d'Alembert (1714–80) and Jean-Jacques Rousseau (1712–78); the 'late Enlightenment' is the time span covered by the generation of Lessing and Kant. Gay defines the programme of the Enlightenment as one of hostility to religion and as the search for 'freedom' and 'progress' achieved by a critical use of reason to change man's relations with himself and society. He emphasises a view of the Enlightenment as virtually that of a liberal reform programme and dwells less on writers such as Rousseau whose works refuse to fit easily into this mould. It is this interpretation which enabled Gay to broaden his canon of thinkers to include the Americans Thomas Jefferson (1743–1826) and Benjamin Franklin (1706–90) and to see the American Revolution of the 1770s, with its commitment to 'Life, Liberty and the pursuit of happiness',[10] as the fulfillment of Enlightenment programmes. Gay's account thus does represent a recognition that Enlightenment was not purely a western European phenomenon, in spite of the strong focus in the rest of his account on developments in France in particular. Nonetheless, Gay's interest in the social context of ideas is minimal at best; as well, like all previous historians of the Enlightenment, Gay's canon of thinkers is exclusively male. Issues of gender, of the different reactions of women to Enlightenment ideas, let alone the Enlightenment's debate on gender itself, are absent from his account.[11]

Gay's synthesis, however, was valuable in encouraging the idea of the Enlightenment as a critical enterprise, committed to engagement with actuality and also as holding diversity within its unity. His synthesis dominated the 1960s. But, by the next decade, lines of analysis which only appear faintly in Gay's account, came increasingly to the fore in the work of other historians. After the publication of H.F. May's *The Enlighten-*

---

[8] Peter Gay, *The Rise of Modern Paganism*, vol. I and *The Science of Freedom*, vol. II (New York, 1966–9).

[9] 'there was only one Enlightenment' (I, 3).

[10] From the preamble to the American Declaration of Independence (4 July 1776).

[11] These issues will be discussed in chapter 4.

1 The frontispiece of the *Encyclopédie* portays reason pulling away
the veil from truth, while clouds withdraw to open up the sky to light.
This title page thus embodies one of the most common readings of the
term 'Enlightenment'.

ment in America[12] it became increasingly difficult to accept a picture of the Enlightenment as 'homogenised', or as occurring only in Europe. For the rest of the Americas, this insight had been anticipated by the publication of A. Owen Aldridge's work on the Enlightenment in the Spanish colonies of the Americas.[13] Aldridge pointed out that accounts like Gay's provided no access into the intellectual world of colonial societies affected by European ideas yet simultaneously surrounded by very different indigenous cultures. Other historians, such as Bernard Plongeron, increasingly repudiated the idea that the Enlightenment had been a movement of 'modern paganism', by pointing to the complex and often far from hostile relationship between the churches and the Enlightenment.[14] Increasingly since the 1970s, the geographical area of 'the' Enlightenment, has enlarged. In particular, the Italian historian Franco Venturi has established Enlightenment as a force on the so-called 'periphery' of Europe: in Italy, Greece, the Balkans, Poland, Hungary and Russia.[15] Venturi's work paid serious attention to the link between Enlightenment ideas, their transmission through newspapers, pamphlets, letters and books and the events which took place in the political sphere. No longer was the Enlightenment able to be seen as an autonomous intellectual movement or as confined to western Europe. In fact, Venturi argued that it was precisely on the 'fringes' of Europe, that stresses and strains within Enlightenment ideas could best be analysed.[16] Venturi was also one of the first historians to discuss a chronology for the Enlightenment which was not linked to the life spans of the great thinkers, but to economic and demographic measurements. In spite of local and national variation, Venturi writes:

in spite of everything, one can hardly fail to recognise a common rhythm among all the local differences ... it is clear that all society, and not just the movement of ideas and politics, is expanding at the beginning of the century, reaches a crisis in the thirties, and reaches its peak in the fifties and sixties, while the last twenty-five years of the century witness a period of profound disturbance. It is the curve of the eighteenth century, and also of the Enlightenment.[17]

---

[12] H.F. May, *The Enlightenment in America* (New York, 1976).

[13] A. Owen Aldridge (ed.), *The Ibero-American Enlightenment* (Urbana, IL., 1971).

[14] Bernard Plongeron, 'Recherches sur L'Aufklärung catholique en Europe occidentale, 1770–1820', *Revue d'histoire moderne et contemporaine*, 16 (1969), 555–605; *Théologie et politique au siècle des lumières 1770–1820* (Geneva, 1973).

[15] Franco Venturi, *The End of the Old Regime in Europe 1768–1776: The First Crisis* (Princeton, 1989). Translated by R. Burr Litchfield, from *Settecento riformatore. III. La prima crisi dell'Antico Regime* (Turin, 1979).

[16] 'It is tempting to observe that the Enlightenment was born and organized in those places where the contact between a backward world and a modern one, was chronologically more abrupt, and geographically closer' (F. Venturi, *Utopia and Reform* (Cambridge, 1971), 133).   [17] Venturi, *Utopia*, 118.

By the 1970s, it was also clear that historians were becoming far more interested in the social basis of the Enlightenment, in the problem of how ideas were disseminated, used and responded to by society. The agenda was no longer the assessment of the work of a restricted number of great writers, in terms of their sources or internal coherence; but was much more turned to looking at *how* ideas were used socially. Simultaneously, there was a far wider recognition that more knowledge was needed not of the great writers, but of the now forgotten authors whose works had often been far more widely accessible in the eighteenth century. The American historian Robert Darnton for example conducted enquiries into social movements such as mesmerism in the Enlightenment, movements conspicuously lacking in 'rationality', but deeply embedded in the sociability of the age.[18] Darnton went on to point out that the majority of books in the Enlightenment had not been produced by great minds, but by now forgotten professional writers, who wrote for a new commercial market in cultural products and who, far from waiting for inspiration or regarding their role as that of a lofty public educator, wrote simply in order to be able to earn enough to eat.[19] Darnton then proceeded to investigate the commercial and economic conditions that made possible the success of the publishing ventures behind some of the 'great works' of the Enlightenment, such as the *Encyclopédie* of Diderot and d'Alembert.[20] It was a natural progression from these new standpoints on the Enlightenment to begin enquiry into the impact of Enlightenment ideas not only in distant geographical areas, but also on social classes far removed from the educated elite. Both Darnton and the French historian Roland Chartier have recently devoted studies to the reception and penetration of the Enlightenment amongst social groups as diverse as peasants and printer's apprentices.[21] Darnton brought to this work another methodological innovation, which was the explicit use of anthropological models drawn from non-European societies, to assess ideas and value systems in the Enlightenment. Darnton alleges that anthropology provides the historian with 'a coherent conception of culture'.[22] Though there has been much debate about the value and appropriateness of such models, their use does

[18] Robert Darnton, *Mesmerism and the End of the Enlightenment in France* (Cambridge, MA, 1968).

[19] Robert Darnton, *The Literary Underground of the Old Regime* (Cambridge, MA, 1982).

[20] Robert Darnton, *The Business of Enlightenment. A Publishing History of the Encyclopédie 1775–1800* (Cambridge, MA, 1979).

[21] Robert Darnton, *The Great Cat Massacre, and Other Episodes in French Cultural History* (New York, 1984); commented upon in Roger Chartier, *Cultural History: Between Practices and Representations* (Ithaca, New York, 1988).

[22] Robert Darnton, 'Intellectual and Cultural History', in Michael Kammen (ed.), *The Past Before Us: Contemporary Historical Writing in the United States* (Ithaca, New York, 1980), 347.

testify to a new willingness among historians to ask new questions of the Enlightenment and to place it in new comparative contexts.

All this change since the days of Cassirer has meant that we now face more than ever a multiplicity of pathways into the study of the Enlightenment. There is now little agreement as to either its chronological or its geographical or social confines, let alone any real interest in defining Enlightenment in terms of a coherent intellectual programme. These problems of definition have been increased by historians' new willingness to question the firm dividing line which used to exist between the study of the Enlightenment and that of the French Revolution.[23] It is now increasingly common to see a continuity throughout the whole eighteenth century, instead of sharply opposing 'the Enlightenment', defined as a concern for progress and rationality, and 'the Revolution', characterised by outbursts of conspicuous bouts of irrationality and violence. Increasingly, therefore, it is the Enlightenment, as much as the French Revolution, which is seen as heralding the coming of a recognisably modern world.

Because of this, it is not only historians who have devoted time to the interpretation of the Enlightenment. Philosophers and political commentators have also reinterpreted it, in the hope of defining the meaning and future of the modern world. The Enlightenment is probably unique among historical movements both in its attracting such interest and in the extent to which such philosophical interpretations have influenced the thinking of professional historians. Among the many post-1945 interpretations of Enlightenment at this interface between philosophy, history and political criticism two in particular stand out. In 1947, firstly, Theodor Adorno and Max Horkheimer published their *Dialectic of Enlightenment*.[24] Writing in the immediate aftermath of a world war and the Holocaust, the authors were concerned to ask 'why mankind, instead of entering into a truly human condition, is sinking into a new kind of barbarism'.[25] This happened, in their view, because of a paradox which lay at the heart of Enlightenment thinking:

the Enlightenment had always aimed at liberating men from fear and establishing their sovereignty. Yet the fully enlightened earth radiates disaster triumphant. The programme of the Enlightenment was the disenchantment of the world: the dissociation of myths and the substitution of knowledge for fancy.[26]

Man gained sovereignty over nature and then over other human beings, by controlling them 'rationally', technologically, which involved a refusal

---

[23] E.g., K.M. Baker, *Inventing the French Revolution: Essays on French Political Culture in the Eighteenth Century* (Cambridge, 1990), especially chapters I and VIII.

[24] *Dialektik der Aufklärung* (Amsterdam, 1947), translated as *Dialectic of Enlightenment* (New York, 1972); all references are from this edition.

[25] *Dialectic*, p. xl.   [26] Ibid., p. 3.

to see nature as the location of mysterious powers and forces which men could not explain.

> Technology ... does not work by concepts and images, by the fortunate insight, but refers to method, the exploitation of others' work and capital. What men want to learn from nature is how to use it in order wholly to dominate it and other men ... On the road to modern science, men renounce any claim to meaning.[27]

Enlightenment, in this view, is ultimately totalitarian in the sense that it abandons the quest for meaning and simply attempts to exert *power* over nature and the world.[28] These insights link Horkheimer's and Adorno's account of the Enlightenment to ideas which are now commonplace in environmental thinking.

According to them, however, the heart of the problem lay in Enlightenment's reliance on 'rationality': that human beings possess the capacity, once released from superstition, mythology and fear, to see solutions to problems which were objectively correct and acceptable to all other 'rational' minds. The problem in practice, as the *Dialectic* points out is that human beings do not in fact agree on what is 'rational'. Since the Enlightenment denies the validity of other ways of arriving at solutions such as tradition, mythology, or religious revelation, it is difficult to resolve these conflicts without the use of force. In other words, lurking at the heart of Enlightenment, is political terror. It was not difficult for the *Dialectic* to develop this point and allege that Enlightenment seemed to have left no legacy which could be used to resist the use of political terror and the technologically assured man-made mass death of the Holocaust, but might even have been at the very heart and origin of these horrors themselves.

Horkheimer and Adorno made two further important points about Enlightenment. In their view, firstly, the Enlightenment project of the 'disenchantment of the world', made it difficult, even where an outward conformity with religion was reached, to focus aspirations of harmony and fulfillment on 'the regions Beyond' but 'transferred them as criteria to human aspiration'.[29] This allowed what the *Dialectic* famously christened 'the administered life', a rational organisation of men, nature and knowledge itself for the achievement of the objectives of this world; the sort of philosophy which makes the idea of 'management' possible. It was this which the *Dialectic* saw as contributing not only to the specific character of everyday life in the twentieth century in the west, but also to the horrors of the concentration camps, where the treatment of human beings as mere objects to be 'administered' and consumed by a 'rational' technological system reached its starkest expression.

The second important idea which the *Dialectic* brought to the study of

[27] Ibid., pp. 3–5.   [28] Ibid., p. 6.   [29] Ibid., p. 87.

the Enlightenment, was that the Enlightenment view of 'rationality' had the effect of turning knowledge into a commodity like any other and thereby of breaking down the area where knowledge and truth, or 'wisedom', were connected. Knowledge and ethics thus also became disconnected. Horkheimer and Adorno argue, that once viewed as a commodity to be bought and sold, knowledge itself became merely a means to an end and 'culture became wholly a commodity disseminated as information without permeating the individuals who acquired it'.[30] These comments again anticipate much which has been said about the impact of the 'information revolution' brought about by computerisation, instantaneous transmission of information and new forms of imaging. Horkheimer's and Adorno's argument that knowledge ceased to be internalised by individual people and became divorced from truth values and hence from ethical questions, will be important to this book's discussion of the growing market place for knowledge in the Enlightenment and the impact of that market place on ideas, or the nature and impact of those ideas themselves. The view of the Enlightenment expressed by Horkheimer and Adorno was thus a profoundly negative one and one which has many resonances with contemporary concerns about man's exploitation of the environment, on the effects of the 'information revolution' and on the likely difficulty of eradicating totalitarianism from European political culture.

Another important interpretation of the Enlightenment, however, is far more positive. The German philosopher and political commentator, Jürgen Habermas is a generation younger than the authors of the *Dialectic*, who were among his own mentors. Like them, he developed his views of the Enlightenment against the background of contemporary concerns. In the 1970s and 1980s, German political life manifested an obvious shift to the right. This shift was accompanied by new attitudes to the German past. The events of the 1930s and 1940s, were newly interpreted by historians sympathetic to the right and often holding important positions in state and federal bureaucracies and policy-making bodies.

Habermas tried to oppose these trends by a re-evaluation of the Enlightenment itself. In his *Structural Transformation of the Public Sphere* (1962), he adopted many of Horkheimer's and Adorno's earlier insights about Enlightenment consumption of culture but without drawing from them the negative conclusions of 1947.[31] For him, other

---

[30] Ibid., p. 197. Alistair MacIntyre, *After Virtue*, 2nd edn (London, 1985), 51–62 argues for similar reasons that the Enlightenment was incapable of providing a secure ground for ethics for future generations.

[31] J. Habermas, *The Structural Transformation of the Public Sphere: An Enquiry into a Category of Bourgeois Society* (Cambridge, MA, 1989), trans. by T. Burger from

potentials of the Enlightenment still made its ideals worth pursuing, to act as correctives to the right wing. Habermas based his view of the Enlightenment on the famous essay by Kant with which we opened this chapter. Habermas emphasised Kant's own perception, that, far from being an epoch which was closed and over, the Enlightenment had still to be pursued and brought to completion. The Enlightenment, he argued, contained the potential of emancipating individuals from restrictive particularism in order to be able to act, not as 'Germans' embattled against the rest of the world by their past and by their adherence to a particular national and cultural ethos, but, rather, as 'human beings', linked to other humans by a common search for universal values such as freedom, justice and objectivity. He thus took on not only his contemporary critics from the right wing, but also German thinkers such as Johann Herder (1744–1803) who even in the eighteenth century had decried Enlightenment attempts to override feelings of distinctiveness due to national identity based on race, religion, language or attachment to the place of birth.

Habermas also argues that the Enlightenment had seen the creation of a 'public realm' for the discussion and transformation of opinions: what we would now call 'public opinion'. In Habermas' view this was created by the middle classes, who organised and consumed the flow of cultural materials and inhabited social structures which determined the transmission of ideas. Far from seeing this, as Horkheimer and Adorno had, as the beginnings of a 'culture industry' which would make 'truth' divorced from 'information' and degrade even the nature of knowledge itself into a purely instrumental search for control, Habermas, on the contrary, saw the creation of the 'public realm' as a means of liberation. For him it meant that 'public opinion' could arise and start to exert influence against privileged traditional forces. Habermas' 'public realm' is a space where men could escape from their role as subjects, and gain autonomy in the exercise and exchange of their own opinions and ideas. Habermas in reinterpreting the culture of the Enlightenment was also demonstrating the possibility of historical analysis filled with moral meaning for the present.

In this his work unexpectedly converged with that of the great French philosopher Michel Foucault who engaged with Habermas in debate over the meaning of the Enlightenment. Like Habermas, Foucault also saw Kant's essay as a crucial definition of Enlightenment. Abandoning earlier positions in which he had seen a great gap between Enlightenment and modern thinking, Foucault took up Kant's view that the Enlightenment

Strukturwandel der öffentlichkeit (Darmstadt, 1962). G. Eley, 'Nazism, Politics and the Image of the Past: Thoughts on the West German *Historikerstreit*', *Past and Present*, 121 (1988), 171–208.

was not complete and used Kant's essay as the starting point for a new understanding of the idea of the critical use of reason as an agent of change. Both thinkers united in agreeing on the importance of the period for a re-evaluation of the present.[32]

Enough has now been said to show the great range of variation in ways of interpreting the Enlightenment. The Enlightenment is unusual in being defined as a movement in thought, rather than as the era of a particular dynasty or of a 'great man'. It is also unusual in the extent to which its historical study has been influenced by analyses inspired by philosophical enquiry. Habermas, Horkheimer and Adorno, not to mention Kant and Hegel, have not only shaped ideas about the basic structures of 'Enlightenment thought', they have also written with the conviction that the Enlightenment is not a 'closed' historical period, but one which, whether for good *or* ill, is still influencing the present; as Kant would have agreed, it is still incomplete. Recent writing on the Enlightenment by professional historians have opened up new areas of enquiry, especially in the social history of ideas, rather than maintaining a concentration on the works of a standard canon of 'great thinkers'. Nor is 'the' Enlightenment any longer seen as a unitary phenomenon. Not only are we now aware of significant national, regional and confessional differences in the Enlightenment experience, but we are also now aware of the different 'Enlightenments' experienced by men and by women, and by white people, and indigenous traditions. All this diversity is hardly surprising, especially when placed against the background of the contemporary inability to define 'the Enlightenment' in any simple way, as the Berlin competition of 1783 made clear.

It might also seem that as our picture of the Enlightenment became more complex, as we have begun to study ideas not as autonomous, discrete objects, but as deeply embedded in society, so the term Enlightenment itself might have become increasingly obscure or even meaningless. It is easy to understand this feeling. A more positive reaction, however, might be to think of the Enlightenment not as an expression which has failed to encompass a complex historical reality, but rather as a *capsule* containing sets of debates, stresses and concerns, which however differently formulated or responded to, do appear to be characteristic of the way in which ideas, opinions and social and political structures interacted and changed in the eighteenth century. This is the

---

[32] Michael Foucault, 'What is Enlightenment?' in Paul Rabinow (ed.), *The Foucault Reader* (New York, 1984), 45–56. Habermas' response is 'Mit dem Pfeil ins Herz der Gegenwart: Zu Foucaults Vorlesung über Kants Was ist Aufklärung?', in J. Habermas, *Die neue Unübersichtlichkeit: kleine politischen Schriften V* (Frankfurt-am-Main, 1985), 126–31; also in D.C. Hoy (ed.), *Foucault: A Critical Reader* (Oxford, 1986), 103–19 as 'Taking aim at The Heart of the Present'.

way in which the Enlightenment will be explored in this book. In order to understand how this interaction could affect so many levels of society and politics, and be present not just in Europe, but throughout most other parts of the world touched by European influence, we turn in the next chapter to explore the new social and economic background to the production, spread and marketing of ideas in this period.

2 Coffee houses and consumers: the social context of Enlightenment

In opulent or commercial society, besides, to think or reason comes to be, like every other employment, a particular business, which is carried on by a very few people, who furnish the public with all the thought and reason possessed by the vast multitudes that labour. Only a very small part of any ordinary person's knowledge has been the product of personal observation or reflection. All the rest has been purchased, in the same manner as his shoes or his stockings, from those whose business it is to make up and prepare for the market that particular species of goods.

(Adam Smith)[1]

Introduction

Recent historical research has focussed overwhelmingly on the social context in which Enlightenment ideas were produced, received and marketed. Historians such as Robert Darnton have produced a wealth of new information on the readers, the writers and the entrepreneurial publishers of the increasingly large number of books, newspapers and pamphlets sold in this period.[2] Historians such as Roger Chartier and Robert Muchembled have examined the penetration of Enlightenment ideas from the elite to the lower social classes, from 'high' to 'low' culture.[3] Others have focussed on the spread of literacy, and the changing nature of the experience of reading.[4] The importance of visual represen-

[1] W.R. Scott, *Adam Smith as Student and Professor* (Glasgow, 1937), 344–5, from draft for the *Wealth of Nations* composed in 1769, and excised from the published text of 1776.
[2] R. Darnton, *The Great Cat Massacre and other Episodes in French Cultural History* (New York, 1984); 'The High Enlightenment and the Low-Life of Literature in Pre-Revolutionary France', *Past and Present*, 51 (1971), 81–115; *The Business of Enlightenment: A Publishing History of the Encyclopédie 1775–1800* (Cambridge, MA, 1979); *The Literary Underground of the Old Regime* (Cambridge, MA, 1982); *Mesmerism and the End of the Enlightenment in France* (Cambridge, MA, 1968).
[3] Roger Chartier, *Cultural History: Between Practices and Representations* (Ithaca, New York, 1988); Robert Muchembled, *Popular Culture and Elite Culture in France, 1400–1750* (London, 1985) translated from his *Culture populaire et culture des élites dans la France moderne* (Paris, 1978).
[4] R.A. Houston, *Literacy in Early Modern Europe* (London, 1988); R. Darnton, 'First Steps towards a History of Reading', *Australian Journal of French Studies*, 23 (1986), 5–30.

tations – pictures, engravings, stage-sets, statues in public places – in the transmission of ideas, alongside the written word, has been closely examined by historians such as Thomas Crow.[5] Many writers have also pointed to the establishment, all over Europe, of new institutions and organisations where ideas could be explored and discussed. Some of these institutions, like masonic lodges, learned academies and societies, were formal affairs, whose membership was carefully controlled.[6] Others, such as public lectures, coffee houses, lending libraries, art exhibitions, operatic and theatrical performances, were nearly all commercial operations, open to all who could pay and thus provided ways in which many different social strata could be exposed to the same ideas.[7] These different media and social institutions focussed on the diffusion and interchange of ideas and together formed what Jürgen Habermas has described as the 'new public sphere' of the eighteenth century.[8] Later in this chapter we will be examining Habermas' ideas more closely and asking what impact, if any, the social setting of ideas produced on the nature of ideas themselves in the Enlightenment.

That social setting, however, was also the result of very large social and political changes in Europe and in the rest of the world. In most areas, especially in Western Europe and North America, the eighteenth century was a time of economic expansion, increasing urbanisation, rising population and improving communications in comparison to the stagnation of the previous century. In some areas of north-west Europe agricultural production also rose significantly. Parts of Britain, the Netherlands and northern Italy entered what historians have decided to call 'the Industrial Revolution'. Production of many goods by artisans in relatively small workshops often under trade guild regulation was replaced for many commodities by production in large factories. Many more objects could be produced in the factories because of increased use of machines to perform tasks hitherto the preserve of skilled human labour. Through

---

[5] Thomas Crow, *Painters and Public Life in Eighteenth-Century Paris* (New Haven and London, 1985).

[6] D. Roche, *Le siècle des lumières en Province: Académies et académiciens provinciaux, 1680–1789* (2 vols.; Paris and The Hague, 1978); M.C. Jacob, *The Radical Enlightenment: Pantheists, Freemasons and Republicans* (London, 1981); N. Hans, 'UNESCO of the Eighteenth Century: La Loge des Neuf Soeurs and its Venerable Master Benjamin Franklin', *Proceedings of the American Philosophical Society*, 97 (1953), 513–24; G. Gayot, *La franc-maçonnerie française. Textes et pratiques, xviiiᵉ–xixᵉ siècles* (Paris, 1980).

[7] By 1760, Vienna alone had at least sixty coffee houses. London and Amsterdam had many more; Crow, *Painters and Public Life*, 104–34; J. Lough, *Paris Theatre Audiences in the Seventeenth and Eighteenth Centuries* (Oxford: Oxford University Press, 1957); R.M. Isherwood, 'Entertainment in the Parisian Fairs of the Eighteenth Century', *Journal of Modern History*, 63 (1981), 24–47.

[8] J. Habermas, *The Structural Transformation of the Public Sphere: An Enquiry into a Category of Bourgeois Society* (Cambridge, MA, 1989): trans. by T. Burger from *Strukturwandel der Offentlichkeit* (Darmstadt, 1962).

2 Electricity provided some of the most spectacular public displays of
scientific principles. Public lectures containing such displays came to
form an integral part of polite culture in the Enlightenment, and
helped to form a large reading market for science. This 'electrified
boy', was a famous showpiece demonstration by the Abbé Nollet. The
boy's body is charged with static electricity by a wheel attached to the
boy's feet. The electricity cannot discharge itself as he is suspended
from above the ground by silken threads, and builds up until his body
attracts objects to it from the stool below him.

'division of labour' every production process was broken down into its smallest components and the skilled craftsman making an entire object from start to finish was to some extent replaced by unskilled labour which was capable of only one small part of that process. This change, whatever its social consequences, enabled greater quantities of consumer goods to be made at lower prices; rising population and better communications enabled these goods to find purchasers and thus boosted manufacturing profits.[9] The increasing volume of goods made and sold included many consumer items such as books, pamphlets, newspapers, pictures, all of which were media for the transmission of ideas and attitudes.[10] Trade in such cultural media between European countries was aided by the increasing practice of translation and also by the fact that in most countries, with the exception of Britain, social elites were trained in the use of French, which in this period almost completely replaced Latin as an international language. It is this increasing trade in cultural media which makes it possible to understand those violent impacts between new ideas and old traditions which Franco Venturi identified as one of the most important ways in which Enlightenment thinking was formed in Europe.[11]

Nor was this trade in cultural media confined to Europe. By the eighteenth century many European states possessed colonial Empires in the Americas, the Caribbean, India and what is now Indonesia. To these colonies, ideas arrived in the trading ships sent out from Europe. Nor was this a one-way traffic, either in commodities or in ideas. Colonial products such as tea, coffee and sugar were vital to the coffee and tea-houses of Europe, where customers met to drink, talk and read the newspapers or the latest books; just as importantly the colonial experience of indigenous cultures was to send back shocks into the Enlightenment in Europe. In the end, the global exchange of ideas, like all market exchanges, broke down barriers between cultural systems, religious divides, gender differences and geographical areas. It promoted a new kind of equality between the 'consumers' of culture, all who could pay for the same book or picture. It also contributed to the increasing homogenisation of the world manifested in the breakdown of indigenous cultural systems and the beginning

[9] P. Mathias, *The First Industrial Revolution*, 2nd edn (London, 1983); M. Berg, *The Age of Manufactures: Industry, Innovation and Work in Britain, 1700–1820* (London, 1985).
[10] N. McKendrick, John Brewer and J.H. Plumb, *The Birth of a Consumer Society: The Commercialisation of Eighteenth-Century England* (London, 1982); T.H. Breen, '"Baubles of Britain": The American and Consumer Revolutions of the Eighteenth-Century', *Past and Present*, 19 (1988), 73–104; G. Barber 'Books from the Old World and for the New: the British International Trade in Books in the Eighteenth-Century', *Studies on Voltaire and the Eighteenth Century*, 151 (1976), 185–224; Darnton, *The Business of Enlightenment*.   [11] See chapter 1.

of the world-wide imposition of the cultural systems generated by Europeans which we are familiar with in the twentieth century. This process of cultural homogenisation continued apace, in spite of the numerous criticisms to which it was subjected at the end of the Enlightenment.[12] In spite of the emergence of forms of cultural nationalism within some European states by the 1790s, European culture when it came into contact with that of indigenous peoples, still had the same effect of causing the collapse of indigenous cultural systems.

In spite of the importance of the visual media and performing arts as vehicles of ideas in this period, it is clear that the printed word occupied a unique position in the transmission of ideas. Books and pamphlets could be easily sold in large numbers, were relatively portable, and could cross language, cultural and geographical boundaries more easily. It is thus important to find out about how and to what extent the printed word was received in the eighteenth century. Historians of literacy, however, have faced notorious problems in estimating how widespread was the ability to read or write. Few historical sources bear directly on this problem and historians have often disputed the very meaning of 'literacy' itself: does it mean fluent reading and writing skills or can its incidence really be indicated, as some have argued, by the numbers of those able to sign their names to surviving formal legal documents?[13] There are additional complications to any such estimates when we realise the great differences in the teaching of reading and writing between our own day and school practice in the eighteenth century. Robert Darnton has pointed out that in Catholic Europe most people were taught to read only to enable them to follow the Latin of the Mass and never gained any fluency in reading the vernacular. Numbers of those affected by elementary schooling are thus not indicators of literacy as we would understand it.[14]

Most of the data that historians use to estimate literacy levels are thus indirect indications, often stemming from social elites. All the indirect indications that we have, however, do point to an increase in the numbers of books, newspapers, journals and pamphlets printed and purchased in this period: and while strictly speaking, this increase does not prove that a greater number of persons in Europe could read and write fluently, it is a finding certainly congruent with that conclusion. Records of book fairs,

---

[12] See chapter 5.
[13] Houston, *Literacy*; François Furet and Jacques Ozouf (eds.), *Reading and Writing: Literacy in France from Calvin to Jules Ferry* (Cambridge, 1982); trans. from *Lire et écrire: L'alphabétisation des français de Calvin à Jules Ferry* (Paris, 1977); contentions that literacy is inherently critical, opening the way to the mobilisation of mass challenge to the existing order, are themselves critically examined in J. Markoff, 'Literacy and Revolt', *American Journal of Sociology*, 92 (1986), 323–49.
[14] Darnton, 'First Steps Towards a History of Reading'.

for example show an increasing number of titles being printed. So do the records of the literary censorships established by many governments, especially in Austria and France.[15] Increasing numbers of libraries were opened to the public, some on a commercial basis, some, like the Royal Library in Paris, being hitherto private institutions. Analysis of wills left by private individuals more frequently mention books among the deceased's possessions, even at quite low social levels.[16] All these indications are fragmentary and it is often hard to make comparisons between different parts of Europe at the same time. Nonetheless, all the indirect indicators point in the same direction: that familiarity with the printed word was spreading throughout society.

Some historians have also argued that the experience of reading itself changed quite dramatically in this period. The German historian Rolf Engelsing has gone so far as to argue that a 'reading revolution' took place by the end of the eighteenth century. Until about 1750, he argues, people read 'intensively'. They possessed only a few books, such as a Bible, devotional works or an almanac; in the English speaking world, Bunyan's *Pilgrim's Progress* was a typical work found among the books of poorer households. These books were read over and over again, sometimes in silence by their owners, but were just as often read aloud to an audience of family and friends. In this way even illiterates gained exposure to the printed word. By the late eighteenth century, Engelsing argues, people were tending to read 'extensively', by which he means reading many printed works once only and then passing quickly on to others. Engelsing also believes that 'extensive' reading was accompanied by an increasing tendency for reading to be done alone, for it to become a solitary, introspective habit, rather than a social one.[17] Insofar as this change penetrated the lower social classes, it made it more difficult for illiterates to have access to the ideas and attitudes carried by the printed word. This is an attractively simple picture, seemingly well able to explain the origins

[15] In 1764, the Leipzig book-fair catalogue included 5,000 titles of newly published books; by 1800 the number had risen to 12,000: Paul Raabe, 'Buchproduktion und Lesepublikum in Deutschland 1770–1780', *Philobiblon*, 21 (1977), 2–16. Similar trends are discernible in France: Robert Estivals, *La statistique bibliographique de la France sous la monarchie au XVIIIè siècle* (Paris and The Hague, 1965); and in colonial North America: G.T. Tanselle, 'Some Statistics on American Printing, 1764–1783', in B. Bailyn and W.B. Hench (eds.), *The Press and the American Revolution* (Boston, 1981), 315–64.

[16] Darnton, 'Towards a History of Reading', 10–12; Daniel Roche, *Le Peuple de Paris: Essai sur la culture populaire au XVIIIè siècle* (Paris, 1981), 204–41; Rudolf Schenda, *Volk ohne Buch. Studien zur Socialgeschichte der populären Lesestoffe, 1700–1910* (Frankfurt-am-Main, 1970), 461–7.

[17] Rolf Engelsing, 'Die Perioden der Lesergeschichte in der Neuzeit. Das statische Ausmass und die Soziokulturelle Bedeutung der Lektüre', *Archiv für Geschichte des Buchwesens*, 10 (1969), cols. 944–1002; *Der Bürger als Leser: Lesergeschichte in Deutschland, 1500–1800* (Stuttgart, 1974).

of our own reading habits today, which are certainly predominantly 'extensive', private and silent. It is also an argument supported by the American historian David Hall, who has described a similar transformation in the reading habits of New Englanders between 1600 and 1850. By the late eighteenth century, New England communities seemed likewise to have abandoned their reliance on a limited repertoire of devotional works and were almost swamped with new genres-novels, newspapers, children's books, travel and natural history – each ravenously absorbed and then discarded for the next.[18] However, it is possible that Engelsing's and Hall's depiction of changes in reading habits is too schematic and based only on small samples of their chosen region. It is also easy to point to much evidence of 'intensive' reading surviving even among the social elites, for example in the many autobiographies which mention obsessional *re*-reading of certain works, and especially of the great best sellers, such as Samuel Richardson's *Pamela* (1740) and *Clarissa* (1747–8), Jean Jacques Rousseau's *Julie ou la Nouvelle Héloïse* (1761) or Johann Wolfgang von Goethe's *Sorrows of Young Werther* (1774).[19] But while there are certainly many indications that the picture is more complex than some historians have maintained, it still does seem, that the late eighteenth century in particular, especially for the upper social classes, was a turning point, a time when more reading material of a more varied character, was eagerly seized upon by a broader reading public than ever before.

No doubt this development was encouraged because physical access to printed materials also became easier in many different ways. The growth of cheap commercial lending libraries allowed many to read 'extensively' who did not possess the financial resources sufficient to build up a large private collection of books. Coffee houses offered newspapers and journals and some of the latest books for the use of customers, for the price of a cup of coffee. Booksellers' shops sometimes also offered light refreshments and a small circulating library for the use of patrons. The very existence of such institutions was dependent on the regular trade in colonial products, on a rising population and the increasing numbers of people living in towns. They also made possible the penetration of ideas expressed in print to both genders and to social strata well outside the elites. This increasing phenomenon was helped by the change in the very nature of the books published. The switch from publishing in Latin to

---

[18] David Hall, 'The Uses of Literacy in New England, 1600–1850', in W.L. Joyce (ed.), *Printing and Society in Early America*, 1–47.

[19] This so-called 'Lesewut' or 'reading fever' is treated in Kurt Rothmann, *Erläuterungen und Dokumente: Johann Wolfgang Goethe: Die Leiden des jungen Werthers* (Stuttgart, 1974); R. Darnton, 'Readers Respond to Rousseau: the Fabrication of Romantic Sensitivity', in *The Great Cat Massacre*, 215–56.

publishing in living languages, helped many to read, particularly women, who lacked the necessary classical schooling to read fluently in Latin. Devotional and theological works seem to have lost their pre-eminent position as reading material. By the late eighteenth century, borrowing patterns in German, English and North American libraries had fallen into strikingly similar patterns. Over 70 per cent of books borrowed fell into the category of novels; 10 per cent for history, biography and travel; less than 1 per cent for religious works.[20] In other words, this period saw the rise of the novel, directly at the expense of theology, as the major vehicle in which readers encountered ideas and attitudes. It is thus not surprising that many Enlightenment novels are as concerned with conveying factual information and discussing controversial points of view as they are in weaving an imaginative narrative structure.[21]

All these changes in reading were necessarily accompanied by profound changes in the social position of writers and publishers. Writers of all countries were often collectively described as belonging to an idealised 'Republic of Letters'. In 1780, the editor of the literary survey the *Histoire de la République des Lettres en France*, described the 'Republic of Letters' as existing:

In the midst of all the governments that decide the fate of men; in the bosom of so many states, the majority of them despotic . . . there exists a certain realm which holds sway only over the mind . . . that we honour with the name Republic, because it preserves a measure of independence, and because it is almost its essence to be free. It is the realm of talent and of thought.

Members of this Republic, he went on, 'form a species by their merit, and gain a reputation as brilliant as that of the great powers of the earth'.[22]

By 1780, these ideas had become commonplace. The idea that writers as knowledge and opinion shapers formed a sort of power which was as formidable as that of organised governments, the idea of equality between all those involved in the Republic of Letters, the values of cosmopolitanism, the idea that knowledge and its producers acted across political boundaries, were all very much to the fore in the Enlightenment.

---

[20] D. Roche, *Les républicains des lettres: Gens de culture et lumières au XVIIIè siècle* (Paris, 1988). Albert Ward, *Book Production, Fiction and the German Reading Public, 1740–1800* (Oxford, 1974); the classic work is still Daniel Mornet, 'Les Enseignments des bibliothèques privées (1750–1780)', *Revue d'histoire littéraire de la France*, 17 (1910), 449–96.

[21] Ian Watt, *The Rise of the Novel* (London, 1957); Michael McKeon, *The Origins of the English Novel, 1660–1740* (Baltimore and London, 1987).

[22] Quoted in L. Daston, 'The Ideal and Reality of the Republic of Letters in the Enlightenment', *Science in Context*, 4 (1991), 367–86 (367–8); from Anon, *Histoire de la République des Lettres en France* (Paris 1780), 5–6. See also S. Neumeister and C. Wiedemann (eds.), *Res Publica Litteraria: Die Institutionen der Gelehrsamkeit in der frühen Neuzeit* (Wiesbaden, 1987).

How far did such ideas correspond to reality? How accurately did they describe the lives and social situations of those who wrote the books, the increased circulation of which fuelled the Enlightenment? This is a topic which has attracted much attention in recent decades and the results of historical research in this field have done much to undermine the older picture of the Enlightenment as the work of a small group of great thinkers. Historians have pointed out that the books most widely read in the Enlightenment were often written by men and women whose names are never mentioned in the canon of great Enlightenment thinkers.[23] These authors were professional writers for a commercial market in the written word, turning out to order books and pamphlets on subjects ranging from political scandal, to pornography, to newspaper articles, book reviews, children's books, novels, theatrical scripts and opera libretti, to retellings of medieval romances for the rural audiences of cheap publishers, to popular science and travel books. It was these writers rather than the elite such as Diderot and Voltaire, who produced the bulk of what was actually read in the Enlightenment. Called collectively 'Grub Street' by Robert Darnton, its very existence demonstrated a great change in the position of writers.[24] Most writers of previous centuries had gained the greater part of their incomes from commissions from personal patrons often drawn from the church, the royal courts or the aristocracy, who often regarded artists and writers in their employment as little more than skilled craftsmen. Such relationships had often involved a high degree of personal and political dependency and social subservience. By the eighteenth century such relationships were very far from over and many, like the musicians Mozart and Haydn, for example, led lives which contained large elements both of personal patronage and of writing for a large commercial audience.[25] But in spite of this incomplete transition, it was still widely felt that a very different social situation was in the process of creation for the producers of ideas and cultural objects and perhaps especially for writers. In the 1740s, for example, the mathematician and thinker Jean d'Alembert (1717–83) was arguing passionately for the independence of men of letters from personal patronage.[26] Such independence was necessary, he argued, if objective, impartial opinions were to be

[23] Daniel Mornet, 'Les Enseignements des bibliothèques privées'.
[24] Darnton, 'The High Enlightenment'; *The Literary Underground of the Old Régime*.
[25] Wolfgang Amadeus Mozart (1756–1791) was at various points under the patronage of the Prince-Bishop of Salzburg until 1781, but also wrote his operas for general performance; Joseph Haydn (1732–1809) spent much of his life under the patronage of the Esterhazy family in Hungary, but also wrote for the open 'market' in music during prolonged stays in London.
[26] Jean d'Alembert, 'Essai sur la société des gens de lettres et des grands, sur la réputation, sur les mécènes, et les récompenses littéraires', in *Mélanges de litteraire, d'histoire et de philosophie* (Amsterdam, 1759).

produced and also to maintain reasonable equality between members of the Republic of Letters. By the 1750s, Denis Diderot (1713–84) could point to the very real existence of such a group of men of letters, which alone, he remarked, made possible the appearance of large collaborative ventures such as the *Encyclopédie* (or Encyclopedia of Arts and Sciences) which he was to publish between 1751 and 1772.[27]

However, the emergence of 'Grub Street', of a distinct community of writers independent from personal patronage, could not in practice guarantee the equality which was one of the ideals of the Republic of Letters. There was little in common in reputation between such well-known thinkers and writers such as Diderot and d'Alembert, who consorted with monarchs and aristocrats, in spite of their lowly social origins, and obscure hacks turning out pot boilers in basements and attics. In terms of income too, there was little comparison between the wealth obtained by some writers such as Voltaire and the precarious existences which Robert Darnton has chronicled for 'Grub Street'. Nor was the Republic of Letters so united in its attitudes towards the powers that be as its idealised description implied. In a controversial article, Darnton has depicted the members of 'Grub Street' as envenomed with envy of the status of the small literary elite, manifesting their alienation from the literary establishment by forceful criticism, which Darnton identifies as one factor leading to the break up of the Old Regime in France and the opening of a revolutionary situation at the close of the century.[28] Whether or not this latter contention is true, it is certain that attacks from 'Grub Street' on the *status quo* were bolder and more direct than much of what issued from the pen of the literary elites – who were often, as for example were Diderot and Voltaire, either paid or pensioned by reigning monarchs, such as the Empress Catherine of Russia (1729–86) or Frederick the Great of Prussia.[29]

There was a further way in which the Republic of Letters was divided: between men and women. Much of this division has its roots in aspects of Enlightenment thinking about gender which will be more fully discussed in chapter 4. More specifically, while there were many women members of 'Grub Street' and even many women belonging to social elites who

---

[27] The *Encyclopédie* has been used by Robert Darnton as a test-case for the commercialised diffusion of the ideas of the Enlightenment: *The Business of Enlightenment*. Diderot noted the importance of a large literary community for the preparation of the *Encyclopédie*: 'you will be obliged to have recourse (rather than to learned societies or famous individuals) to a large number of men of different sorts and conditions – men of genius to whom the gates of the academies are closed by reason of their low rank in the social scale': entry *Encyclopédie*, reprinted in K.M. Baker, *The Old Régime and the French Revolution* (Chicago and London, 1987), 71–89, esp. 74. [28] Darnton, 'The High Enlightenment'.
[29] This range of responses to the *status quo* in government and society, from the supportive to the critical, will be examined in greater depth in chapters 7 and 8.

pursued ideas, such as Voltaire's own companion, the Marquise Emilie du Châtelet (1706–49), there was at the same time a concerted attack by many male writers on the capacity of women in general to contribute to the store of ideas and discussions.[30] Often these attacks came down to the idea, forcefully stated in Rousseau's educational tract *Emile* (1762), that woman was a creature whose physical make up ensured that she was ruled by emotion, rather than rationality, fitted by her biology to be only the mate and helper of men and dominated by her reproductive function.[31] Why was this attack on women's rationality, her very capacity to think, so strong a feature of the allegedly egalitarian Republic of Letters? In Rousseau's *Emile*, Sophie, the female protagonist who was presented as Emile's ideal mate, is so precisely because she is excluded by her femininity from the education which it is the book's entire purpose to define for Emile. The reasons for this are explored in much greater detail elsewhere in this book. But, in social terms, part of the problem may have come from the insecurity of the intellectual class itself. Still completing the transition from hired dependent of the great to autonomous intellectual producer, the Republic of Letters yet laid claim to be a political force in its own right, capable of building and moulding 'public opinion', in a way which obeyed, in theory, the dictates of reason, impartiality and humanity, and just as powerfully as could established governments. Because of this, the autonomy of knowledge producers was a crucial issue: how could they lay claims to be the legitimate builders of the opinions of the public, if they were not themselves independent and impartial? By definition, to most eighteenth-century people, women could never be independent or autonomous, because of their family duties, or impartial, because of their emotional natures. The participation of women was thus seen as reducing the legitimacy of the Republic of Letters as a whole. Their equivocal position, as knowledge producers who were never truly accepted as part of the Republic of Letters, demonstrates how, in spite of its universalism, the Enlightenment itself often seemed to devote as much energy to designating entire social groups, such as women or peasants, as impervious to the voice of reason, as it did to constructing a better world for human beings.

In examining other crucial institutions in the spread of Enlightenment ideas, it is probably more accurate to see such institutions as effective ways of producing unity between elite groups in society, rather than

[30] Jocelyn Harris, 'Sappho, Souls and the Salic Law of Wit', in A.C. Kors and P.J. Korshin, *Anticipations of the Enlightenment in England, France and Germany* (Philadelphia, 1988), 232–58.
[31] Maurice M. Bloch and Jean H. Bloch, 'Women and the Dialectics of Nature in Eighteenth-Century French Thought', in C.P. MacCormack and M. Strathern (eds.), *Nature, Culture and Gender* (Cambridge, 1980), 25–41.

reaching out to other, unprivileged social groups, In Britain, for example, extensive literacy and a large and wealthy professional and commercial middle class, produced institutions which were aimed at the discussion of ideas, and whose membership of local elites also helped those elites to meet on common, neutral ground and forge firmer contacts with each other. Among such societies could be mentioned the Manchester Literary and Philosophical Society, founded in 1785 and still in existence, or the 'Lunar Society', a Birmingham-based group including the industrialist Josiah Wedgwood, the poet and doctor Erasmus Darwin, grandfather of the naturalist, and the inventor Joseph Arkwright,[32] which well illustrates how a common interest in Enlightenment ideas could produce a new social institution able to produce a new interplay between manufacturers, men of science and local intellectuals. All these groups meeting for discussion and experimentation were new forms of sociability centering on the exchange of ideas, social institutions where distinctions among different members were temporarily abandoned in the impartial search for truth and the pursuit of ideas.

This emphasis on equality was carried even further in another social institution, that of Freemasonry. Throughout Britain and Europe, Masonic lodges flourished, and saw the heavy involvement of aristocrats and even reigning princes such as Frederick the Great of Prussia, and Francis I of Austria, in the central European lodges. Their membership, which was supposed to be secret, vowed to cast aside social distinctions and unite their memberships with pledges to the practical fulfilment in society of key Enlightenment ideas such as rational benevolence. Masonic lodges, some of which were open to women, became centres of debate where members tried to understand the world in ways which were often tinged with mysticism and which sought the moral regeneration of society and individuals without reference to established religions. Mozart's opera, *The Magic Flute* (1791) with its extensive use of Masonic imagery, is one of the highest artistic expressions of this ideal. In some parts of Europe however, Masonry attracted hostility. It was condemned by the Catholic church. In some German states, its programme of total social regeneration and its secrecy laid Masonry open to misinterpretation, as a challenge to the social and political status quo, especially as some Masons were also members of secret societies such as the Illuminati, which aimed to establish their members as a new ruling order. The movement frequently, therefore met a hostile reception, especially as political tensions climbed towards the end of the century. In these contexts, Masonry illustrated the central dilemma of the Enlightenment: having

[32] R.E. Schofield, *The Lunar Society of Birmingham* (Oxford, 1963).

created 'opinion' as a new political force, how far was it practicable or justifiable to use that force to produce social and political change.[33]

In France and Italy, different institutions were to the fore in promoting debate on Enlightenment ideas and bringing together old and new sections of the elite. Learned Academies were founded in many provincial towns in this period. These were formally organised bodies, often with constitutions laid down by royal charters and usually possessing their own premises and library. Membership was open to those who could pay a fee, which in practice meant the local elites: the aristocracy, the higher members of royal and ecclesiastical bureaucracies, the commercial elites, the wealthier members of professions such as medicine and the military. They existed to promote debate, to comment on papers on learned or topical subjects presented by their members, to encourage intellectual life by providing a library and in the case of the wealthier institutions, to launch and finance prize essay competitions.[34] The prize essays, once reprinted, were capable of mobilising public opinion far beyond the confines of Academy membership, as witness to the furious public debates which took place on the subject of capital punishment, after the prize competition at the Academy of Metz in 1784, or on the social role of the Arts, after an equally renowned competition at Dijon in 1750.[35] Such institutions, as their historian Daniel Roche has remarked, performed not only valuable intellectual roles, but also helped in bringing together the social elites, both new and traditional, of each region and making them part of the new force of 'public opinion'.[36]

[33] Reinhard Koselleck, *Critique and Crisis: Enlightenment and the Pathogenesis of Modern Society* (Oxford, New York and Hamburg, 1988), translated from *Kritik und Krise. Eine Studie zur Pathogenese der bürgerlichen Welt* (Freiburg and Munich, 1959), 86–97.

[34] The provincial Academies in France have been studied in D. Roche, *Le Siècle des lumières en province. Académies et académiciens provinciaux, 1680–1789* (2 vols., Paris and The Hague, 1978). Many other academies, such as the Royal Society of London and the Academy of Sciences in Paris, were more formally organised under direct royal control in the late seventeenth and eighteenth centuries: Roger Hahn, *Anatomy of a Scientific Institution: the Paris Academy of Sciences 1666–1803* (Berkeley, CA., 1971); James E. McClellan III, *Science Reorganised: Scientific Societies in the Eighteenth Century* (New York, 1985). Societies devoted to economic reform and development are discussed in the classic work of Robert J. Shafer, *The Economic Societies in the Spanish World, 1763–1821* (Syracuse, 1958).

[35] The Metz competition was won by Pierre-Louis Lacretelle, 'Discours sur les peines infamantes, couronné à l'Académie de Metz, en 1784, et ensuite à l'Académie française, en 1785, comme l'ouvrage le plus utile de l'année', in P-L. Lacretelle, *Oeuvres Diverses* (3 vols., Paris, an X, 1802), I, 171–329. The future French Revolutionary leader Robespierre was runner-up. The Dijon competition was won by Rousseau with a *Discours sur les Sciences et les Arts* which sparked immediate public debate. Texts relating to the Berlin Academy of Sciences competition of 1780, are discussed in chapter 2, note 4.

[36] For discussion of this concept in the Enlightenment see Habermas, *Structural Transformation*, 89–117. In French, the term was first used by Rousseau in his 1750 *Discours*: J.J. Rousseau, 'Discourse on the Sciences and Arts (First Discourse)', in R.D. and J.R.

But in all this debate about the social institutions and social impact of the Enlightenment we have so far been concentrating on the experience of social elites: of those who were literate, who could afford to pay for membership of an Academy club, or Masonic lodge, or the purchase of a cup of coffee in a coffee shop, or the membership fee of a circulating library. Overwhelmingly, therefore, we have also been discussing an urban population. We now have to turn to the opposite side of the social divide. How far and with what means, did Enlightenment ideas penetrate into social classes outside the elites and outside the towns; into the rural populations which in most European countries still made up the vast majority of the population? This is a topic which certainly exercised contemporaries.[37] It is also one which has attracted increasing attention from historians in recent years, as has every other aspect of the social history of the Enlightenment. This interest sprang into prominence beginning in 1975, with several studies of the *Bibliothèque Bleue*, the collection of small-sized, cheaply produced and crudely illustrated books produced for a semi-literate rural market by the Oudot firm of printers and publishers based in the French town of Troyes.[38] Sold in large numbers at country fairs and cheap booksellers, these books included almanachs with farming advice and weather predictions, sensational biographies of famous criminals, condensed versions of recent novels, devotional works, and in the great majority, retellings of medieval romances telling the deeds of Roland, the chevalier Bayard, or the four sons of Aymon. Literary historians have seen this literature as purely escapist, even as a way in which poor folk were deliberately deprived of access to Enlightenment debate. Others such as Bollème, have seen the *Bibliothèque Bleue* as evolving towards increasing harmony with Enlightenment thinking. But to view the *Bibliothèque Bleue* in this way is to oversimplify the complexities of the relationships between what historians have sometimes called 'high' and 'low' culture: the culture of the mass of the population and the elites. Even setting aside the notorious problems which have surrounded the definition of the word 'culture', there is much evidence for an interpenetration of cultural reference points

Masters (eds.), *The First and Second Discourses* (New York, 1964), 50. By the 1730s, the term was current in English meaning the articulation of personal rational reflection, through the public clash of argument. The term is first documented in English in 1781 by the *Oxford English Dictionary*.

[37] Many writers were concerned that their works should *not* reach the lower social classes; Diderot wrote to his publisher 'There are ... some readers whom I don't want and never shall; I write only for those with whom I could talk at my ease' (quoted in J-P. Belin, *La mouvement philosophique de 1748 à 1789* (Paris, 1913), 73).

[38] G. Bollème, *La Bibliothèque Bleue: littérature populaire en France aux XVIIᵉ et XVIIᵉ siècles* (Paris, 1980); R. Mandrou, *De la culture populaire en France aux XVIIᵉ et XVIIᵉ siècles. La bibliothèque bleue de Troyes* (Paris, 1964).

between social classes; at the same time as the *Bibliothèque Bleue* for example, peddled retold medieval romance to its humble readership, such romances were also being sold to the upper-class readership of the *Bibliothèque Universelle des Romans*, initiating what literary historians have called a 'Gothic Revival'.[39] It should also not be forgotten that the largest single occupational group in most cities was composed of domestic servants, who often came from rural communities. Living in enforced intimacy with their employers, we can posit that their role in 'transmission' between town and country, peasants and urban employers, was of considerable importance in breaking down any hard and fast divisions between 'high' and 'low' culture, or rural and urban worlds, and this role of 'transmission' was enhanced by the expansion in western Europe at least, of postal services which enabled even the minimally literate to communicate their experiences and ideas to each other.[40] This picture has been supported by the work of Roger Muchembled, who sees the end of the eighteenth century as a time of great cultural convergence. Muchembled pinpoints the lower-middle class in France in particular as an area where 'high' and 'low' cultures mingled.[41] Other historians of culture in this period, such as Roland Chartier, emphasise the very severe problems in the way of anyone who tries to get behind literary and artistic images of peasants and workers, to find what their real reading and thinking were. Chartier's studies seem to reveal a largely traditional world, in which a rural population remained relatively unaffected by the ideas of the Enlightenment.[42] A similar picture emerges from Robert Darnton's portrayal of the mind set of urban apprentices in Paris.[43] Both these historians, in spite of many conflicts between them, in fact present a picture of the social penetration of Enlightenment thinking which is very close to a certain strand of opinion in the Enlightenment itself. Many Enlightenment reformers approached the rural population in a way which

---

[39] The *Bibliothèque Universelle des Romans* was published between 1775 and 1789 and owed much to the medieval adaptations of the Comte de Tressan (1705–83).

[40] Beaumarchais' Figaro (the original of the Mozart opera character) could not have been the only gentleman's valet in the 1780s to be familiar with some of the latest ideas. In Philadelphia, shopkeepers and craftsmen were members of the American Society for Promoting and Propagating Useful Knowledge, the forerunner of the American Philosophical Society. Pictures were also a powerful means of conveying Enlightenment ideas. William Hogarth (1697–1764), the great British artist, for example designed his 1751 series of engravings *The Four Stages of Cruelty*, an eloquent attack on cruelty to animals, specifically for the working class. See R. Paulson, *Hogarth*, vol. II (New Haven and London, 1971), 109.

[41] Robert Muchembled, *Culture populaire et culture des élites dans la France moderne* (Paris, 1977).

[42] Roger Chartier, 'Figures of the Other: Peasant Reading in the Age of the Enlightenment', in *Cultural History*, 151–71; and in *Dix-huitième siècle*, 18 (1986), 45–64.

[43] Darnton, *The Great Cat Massacre*, especially the title study.

reminds us of the way missionaries in the following century would regard indigenous peoples. They saw peasants as beings living almost in a different world, incapable of understanding the Enlightenment and buried instead in incomprehensible folk superstitions, irrational traditions and religious loyalties.[44] To break down the peasants' resistance to Enlightenment was one of the major objectives of Enlightenment social reformers; but it was a task which, simultaneously, they often despaired of completing.[45] In the divergence between Darnton, Chartier and Muchembled, we probably simply have to conclude that the jury is still out: the vastness of the subject, the difficulty of international comparisons, the problematic distinctions involved in defining 'high' and 'low' culture, and the comparative scarcity and intractability of the evidence, mean that in all likelihood no resolution of this problem, as it is presently defined, is probable. All that we can conclude is that the very complexity of historical interpretation on this subject might well itself reflect a flexible and ambiguous reality of the social penetration of Enlightenment thinking. It should also remind us that ideas, reference points and attitudes did not simply 'trickle down' from the literary and intellectual elites to the deprived masses; movement may well have occurred in the opposite direction.

Conclusion

The Enlightenment was an era where dramatic shifts occurred in the production and accessibility of ideas and especially in the case of print media. New social institutions were constructed based on the interchange of ideas, rather than to mark or display social and political rank. Knowledge and the ability to debate ideas in public began to be one of the ways of acquiring status for those born outside aristocratic elites. Simultaneously, a world-wide trade developed in consumer goods, including portable cultural products such as books, newspapers, pamphlets and reproductions of paintings. Increasingly, culture became 'commodified', a development explored in the philosophical analysis of Enlightenment by Horckheimer and Adorno, which has been previously referred to. The rendering accessible of information and debates to a wide audience became big business and was carried out not only by the elite of Enlightenment thinkers, but by an army of professional writers whose names are now largely forgotten. Visual representations and performance

---

[44] Harvey Mitchell, 'Rationality and Control in French Eighteenth-Century Medical Views of the Peasantry', *Comparative Studies in Society and History*, 21 (1979), 81–112; D. Outram, *The Body and the French Revolution* (New Haven and London, 1989), 41–67.
[45] See chapter 7.

arts also carried ideas to wide audiences outside the social elites. All this led to the emergence of 'public opinion' as a force to be reckoned with. Indeed, a second major paradox of the Enlightenment is the way in which public opinion as a critical political force was brought into being at the same time, and through many of the same social and economic mechanisms through which culture also became part of an international system of trading and exchange. Did commodification itself create the public realm? That too is a question on which the jury is still out.

Nonetheless, as Daniel Roche has pointed out, the growth of 'public opinion' also itself raised a third fundamental problem: that of defining the real elite. Was it that of birth or that of intellect? Questions of the control and spread of knowledge and ideas became part of the uneasy relationships between social classes; it also became part of the relationships between states and societies, monarchies and social classes.

3   The rise of modern paganism?
Religion and the Enlightenment

> The greatest number still believe that the Enlightenment is concerned with almost nothing but religion.   (Johann Pezzl)

> When all prejudice and superstition has been banished, the question arises: Now what? What is the truth which the Enlightenment has disseminated in place of these prejudices and superstitions?
> (Georg Wilhelm Friedrich Hegel)

> I knew a real theologian once ... He knew the Brahmins, the Chaldeans ... the Syrians, the Egyptians, as well as he knew the Jews; he was familiar with the various readings of the Bible.... The more he grew truely learned, the more he distrusted everything he knew. As long as he lived, he was forebearing; and at his death, he confessed he had squandered his life uselessly.   (Voltaire)[1]

As we have seen, 'Enlightenment' is a term which has been defined in many different ways both by contemporaries and by later historians. But nowhere is the divergence between contemporary and later definitions wider than in the area of religion. Until recently, few historians would have echoed Johann Pezzl's contemporary judgement on the centrality of religious issues to the Enlightenment. Indeed, in the nineteenth century, many conservative historians saw the Enlightenment as a time characterised by deliberate efforts to undermine religious belief and organisations. Some went so far as to link anti-religious attitudes fostered by the Enlightenment with the outbreak of the French Revolution itself in 1789 (see chapter 8). This is a view taken also by many modern historians. It is Peter Gay who significantly subtitles one volume of his synthetic study of the Enlightenment as the 'rise of modern paganism'. Similarly, Keith Thomas has seen the eighteenth century as a time of 'disenchantment of the world', meaning the collapse of a way of seeing the world as full of magical or spiritual powers and forces organising a mysterious cosmos.

---

[1] Johann Pezzl, *Marokkanische Briefe* (Frankfurt and Leipzig, 1784), 174–5; G.W.F. Hegel, *Phänomenologie des Geistes* (ed.), Johannes Hoffmeister (Hamburg, 1952), 397. English version, *The Phenomenology of Mind*, trans. J.B. Baillie (New York and Evanston, 1967), 576; Voltaire, *Philosophical Dictionary* (1764), article 'Theologian'.

Thomas argues that this change in religious values had very important consequences. From being seen as a power moving outside and beyond the created world, God, he argues, 'was confined to working through natural causes' and 'obeyed natural laws accessible to human study'.[2] While Thomas is certainly not arguing that the Enlightenment saw an end of religious belief, he is arguing for a radical shift in religious conceptions from the beginning of the eighteenth century. Nor is this perception of the Enlightenment as a time of the decline of supernatural, 'mysterious' religion, confined to English-speaking historians. Michel Vovelle has also seen a slow decline in religious belief, which he somewhat dramatically describes as 'dechristianisation' in the south of France, which he finds evidenced by the declining use of religious phrases in wills, and declining numbers of bequests with religious objectives. In spite of the controversy his work has attracted, mainly due to his choice of sources, it has seemed nevertheless attractive to many because it seems to point to a connection between declining religious belief pre-1789, and the attempts made during the French Revolution both to stamp out Christian belief in France, and to produce new forms of 'rational' or 'natural' religion.[3]

Gay, Vovelle and Thomas, have thus all produced work arguing that the Enlightenment saw either an absolute decline in religious belief, or a radical shift in its meaning and context. Nor is this a new view of the Enlightenment. Genealogy for this view is provided not merely by the conservative historians who considered the relationship between Enlightenment and Revolution in the previous century. It is also supported by the contemporary analysis of the impact of the Enlightenment on religion by the great German philosopher, G.W.F. Hegel (1770–1831), many of whose arguments on this point are also adopted by Horkheimer's and Adorno's *Dialectic of Enlightenment*.[4] Hegel's analysis pinpoints religious issues as indicative of fundamental shifts in Enlightenment thought. For Hegel, the Enlightenment, especially in France, was an inherently religious movement, where the *philosophes* 'carried out the Lutheran Reformation in a different form'. For him, both Reformation and Enlightenment were contributions to the same objective, that of human spiritual freedom: 'What Luther had initiated in the heart, was freedom of spirit.' Nonetheless, Hegel argued that the Enlightenment had mistaken its path, in arguing that faith should be assessed by rationality. Hegel is also concerned that attacks by *philosophes* on the reality of spiritual experience also rely on the idea that all real ideas

---

[2] Keith Thomas, *Religion and the Decline of Magic: Studies in Popular Belief in Sixteenth and Seventeenth-Century England* (London, 1983), 640, 659.

[3] Michelle Vovelle, *Piété baroque et déchristianisation en Provence au XVIIIᵉ siècle: Les attitudes devant la mort d'après les clauses des testaments* (Paris, 1973).

[4] Horkheimer and Adorno, *Dialectic of Enlightenment* (New York, 1972).

ultimately come only from sense experience. For Hegel this meant that the Enlightenment, instead of completing its historical mission to complete the Reformation, was in severe danger of destroying faith altogether. In doing so, it would, according to Hegel, be destroying a crucial aspect of man's self-knowledge, its relation to the absolute and the spiritual

Formerly, they had a heaven adorned with a vast wealth of thoughts and imagery. The meaning of all that is, hung on the thread of light by which it was linked to that of heaven. Instead of dwelling in this world, presence, men looked beyond it, following the thread to an other-wordly presence, so to speak. The eye of the spirit had to be forcibly turned and held fast to the things of this world; and it has taken a long time before the lucidity which only heavenly beings used to have could penetrate the dullness and confusion in which the sense of worldly things was enveloped, and so make attention to the here and now as such, attention to what has been called 'experience', an interesting and valid enterprise. Now, we seem to heed just the opposite: sense is so fast rooted in earthly things that it requires just as much force to raise it. The Spirit shows itself so impoverished that, like a wanderer in the desert craving for a mouthful of water, it seems to crave for its refreshment only the bare feelings of the divine in general.

Furthermore, Hegel alleged that the Enlightenment failed to produce any set of beliefs which could possibly replace religious faith. Enlightenment had in fact, he thought, changed the grounds of debate about religion away from questions of religious/theological *truth*, which obsessed the Reformation era of the sixteenth and seventeenth centuries, to become equally obsessed with the utility of religion, in the sense of providing social stability. Alternatively, according to Hegel, the Enlightenment simply saw religion as an outcrop of other phenomena such as the laws of nature, which were knowable by man. In any case, religion ceased to have an independent status as relating to a world of faith only partially knowable by man, and became totally assimilated to the human needs and human understanding. Once man became an end in himself, as Hegel alleged he was in Enlightenment thought, once he lost religious aspiration, then he becomes trapped in his own solipsism, unable to judge himself aright, or to form non-utilitarian ties to other human beings. Thus, Hegel like Kant saw the Enlightenment as an uncompleted project for intellectual and spiritual freedom. But for Hegel, the Enlightenment had betrayed itself, left unfulfilled its religious mission, because of the nature of the image of man which it produced, which emphasised human autonomy and self-sufficiency.[5]

---

[5] This analysis is considerably indebted to Lewis Hinchman, *Hegel's Critique of The Enlightenment* (Gainesville, Florida, 1984), chapter 5. See also H.R. Trevor-Roper, 'The Religious Origin of the Enlightenment', in his *Religion, Reformation and Social Change*, 3rd edn. (London, 1984). Quotation from Hegel, *Phenomenology of Spirit*, translated A.V. Miller (Oxford, 1977), 5.

These are views of the relationship betwen Enlightenment and religion which have been enormously influential. Nor was Hegel's view of the religious thought of the Enlightenment without considerable substance, especially in the case of France. Religious movements such as Deism, especially strong in Britain and France, denied that man could gain any knowledge of the Creator apart from the mere fact of 'his' existence. Writers such as Voltaire alternately crusaded against all organised religion, or argued that religious observance was only to be tolerated because of its utility in producing social stability, not because its claims were actually true. Materialists such as Julien de la Mettrie (1709–51) argued in his *L'Homme Machine* of 1747 that there was no such thing as a soul, and that all knowledge came ultimately from sense impressions of the surrounding physical world.[6] Men, the baron d'Holbach argued in another notorious materialist treatise, the *Système de la Nature* (1771), should abandon religion completely, to reconcile themselves with 'nature'.[7] And again, economic thought in the Enlightenment in the works of such men as Adam Smith, did define individuals as autonomous seekers of self-interest rather than of salvation.

However, our picture of the Enlightenment as 'modern paganism' starts to become considerably more complex once we abandon this focus on the small group of determinedly anti-religious thinkers who are almost confined to the French Enlightenment. As we have already seen, thinkers of the stature of Hegel saw the Enlightenment as a movement which could not be understood except within religious categories, however one assesses his claim that the Enlightenment had betrayed man's religious nature. In fact the Enlightenment produced a wide variety of responses to organised religion, ranging all the way from violent Voltairean hostility to religion, through to attempts to bolster orthodox belief by demonstrating its rationality and accordance with natural law. The century can also be seen as one of great religious creativity, even creating the characteristic and new religious idea, that of toleration, which was possibly its most important legacy to succeeding centuries. The Enlightenment saw not only attempts to stabilise orthodox belief by demonstrating its acceptability to human reason, but also powerful religious movements, such as English Methodism, the 'Great Awakening' in the North American colonies, the rise of the mystical sect known as Hassidism within Polish Judaism, and the Pietist movement in the German states, which all emphasised a personal and emotional faith. Religious controversy within

---

[6] Julien Offray de la Mettrie, *L'Homme Machine* (Paris, 1747), ed. Paul Laurent Assoun (Paris, 1981).

[7] Paul-Henri Thomas D'Holbach, *Système de la Nature ou des lois du monde physique et du monde moral* (Paris, 1769).

Christianity and Judaism also had a powerful reciprocal impact on the development of historical scholarship in this period, involving a complete reworking of thinking about the historical development of human society. At the same time, Deism, the belief that little or nothing could be known about the creator except the fact of his existence as a precondition for that of the workings of the natural laws governing the cosmos, posed in an acute form the relationship between science and religion. The century is one of powerful multivarious religious debate and innovation, which certainly cannot be encapsulated in Voltaire's famous battle-cry of *Ecrasez l'infâme*: wipe out the infamy of organised religion.

Let us turn first to that most characteristic Enlightenment idea: that of the importance of religious toleration. Though some voices had been raised, particularly in England and France, in the seventeenth century on the side of toleration, it was to be the eighteenth century which saw the determining debates and decisions on this issue. Indeed in terms of religion, the century of the Enlightenment can be seen as framed by two important measures for toleration: in 1689 the English Parliament passed the Toleration Act in Great Britain, which greatly decreased (without altogether removing) legal penalties against those who did not subscribe to the Church of England, especially Catholics and Dissenters. In 1787, the monarchy in France issued decrees allowing limited toleration and some lessening of civil disabilities to Protestants. In between these two decrees lay a long period of struggle and argument over the issue.

Why should the issue of religious toleration have aroused such strong passions, and such continuous debate in the Enlightenment? This happened to a large extent because the Enlightenment was also heir to the Reformation in a different sense to that understood by Hegel. It was the heir not only to its potential legacy of intellectual freedom, but also to the military and political conflicts, which had been aroused by Luther's attempts to reform the Catholic church in the sixteenth century. From the sixteenth century until the Peace of Westphalia in 1648, states whose rulers were of opposing religious convictions had fought each other, at least partly to impose their religious convictions on their opponents. At the same time, as conflict broke out between states, religious dissent proliferated *within* states. Catholic states, such as France, produced embattled Protestant minorities. Protestant states, such as England, persecuted Catholics, and faced a proliferation of mutually hostile Protestant sects within their own borders. Such internal religious conflict was fertile ground for foreign intervention. In both the Protestant and Catholic camps it was widely held that error had no rights, and that those who held religious views which differed from those of the reigning monarch were disloyal subjects whose very existence challenged the unity and stability of state and society. To a large extent, the Enlightenment's attempts to come to grips with the issue of toleration, was also an attempt to confront its immediate past and to influence future outcomes. Enlightenment thinkers grappled with a past full of religious intolerance with the same urgency that the late twentieth century has grappled with the issues raised by the Holocaust.

Some of this began to change when Westphalia brought to a close a prolonged period of warfare in Europe, known as the Thirty Years' War, some of whose most important causes were to be found in hostility between Catholic and Protestant states. The year 1648 saw the end of war *between* states with the objective of enforcing religious allegiances. Some rulers still were to attempt to impose religious uniformity *within* their own borders, for, of course, the prolonged religious conflict before 1648 had not produced religious homogeneity within *any* state. But the changed international situation meant that the confessions and the dynasties were no longer so embattled over the religious issue. In the eighteenth century, states were increasingly faced with real decisions as to whether to continue to strive for confessional uniformity within their own borders, or whether to tolerate religious diversity, and, if so, to what extent. At the same time, a rising tide of opinion looked back with revulsion at the devastation and chaos caused by religious conflict between and within states in the past. Was conflict and instability too high a price to pay for religious uniformity? Increasingly, it was also pointed out that religious belief could not in any case be compelled. Religious belief was increasingly seen as something that should not dominate man like a foreign power, but freely arise from interior forces such as conscience and reason. Thus attempts to impose uniformity by force were nonsensical.

Nonetheless, in spite of this rising tide of opinion in favour of religious toleration, manifested for example in Voltaire's 1763 *Traîte de la tolérance*, it was not easy for many rulers to take decisive steps towards legally implementing it. Religious toleration, which seems so obviously acceptable to us, in fact raised many issues about the nature of state and monarchy, which were not easy to resolve. The victory for religious toleration was thus not immediate or speedy, as the gap of a century between the Toleration Act in Britain and the Toleration Decrees in France should remind us.

For many, toleration posed as many problems as it answered. How could subjects of a faith different from that of the ruler or the established church, be seen as truly loyal? How could they take binding oaths? How far would the extension of religious toleration change the nature of state and monarchy? This was a particularly important question at a time when the great majority of states were governed by monarchies whose legitimacy stemmed at least in part from their claims to allegiance to a particular church. To give only a few examples the French monarch, whose subjects included a sizeable number of Protestants, took a coronation oath to extirpate heresy. The English monarch was secular head of the Church of England. The King of Prussia was *summus episcopus* of the Lutheran church. Thus, at stake in the struggle for state-supported religious toleration was a transition from the idea of a monarchal state as necessarily involving also a uniform community of believers, to the idea of an impersonal state where religious loyalties could be separated from loyalty to the state itself: in other words, the transition from a distinctively *ancien regime* political order to one more typically modern. This was not a particularly attractive option, for example, for a ruler like Maria Theresa of Austria who saw her role as that of acting as a specifically *Catholic* monarch and was willing to deport many thousands of her Bohemian Protestant subjects in order to work still towards the creation of a uniformly Catholic state.

This was an issue about which there were thus great variations of viewpoint. Maria Theresa and her son and successor Joseph II, for example, held strongly opposing views on the issue of toleration, views which reflected different ideals about the nature of a modern polity, and thus of the role of the ruler. Joseph wanted to be able to define his subjects apart from their religious allegiance, Maria Theresa looked for a polity which still had something to do with the ideal of a unified Christendom which the Reformation had broken down. Opposing each other here were two different world views.[8] Each possessed valid arguments; neither of them was negligible.

Thinking about toleration thus did not have foregone conclusions. While Maria Theresa (1717–80) and Joseph II (1741–90) struggled over the issue, their contemporary Frederick II (1712–86) of Prussia, who came to the throne in 1740, the same year as Maria Theresa, adopted a quite different line on the issue. In spite of the fact that Frederick was *summus episcopus* within the majority Lutheran church in Prussia, he established policies of wide religious toleration within his kingdom, immediately on his accession. Frederick defined his functions as holding the ring between the many different religious groups in Prussia, to the extent of even allotting state funds for the building of a new Catholic Cathedral in his capital city, Berlin, in 1747. Heresy enquiries, and public

---

[8] Joseph II wrote to Maria Theresa in June 1777, 'with freedom of religion, one religion will remain, that of guiding all citizens alike to the welfare of the state. Without this approach we shall not save any greater number of souls, and we shall lose a great many more useful and essential people'. A. von Arneth, *Maria Theresa und Joseph II: Ihr Correspondenz* (2 vols., Vienna, 1864), II, 141–2.

exposition of theological controversy were forbidden. In 1750, a revised General Privilege and Regulation for the Jews in Prussia increased Jewish rights, though not to the level of full toleration, though they were given the right to be tried by their own laws, and given the possession of their own schools, cemeteries and synagogues. Religious toleration was enforced in the Prussian army. As Frederick – who was personally an unbeliever – put it in a famous letter of June 1740: 'All must be tolerated ... here everyone must be allowed to choose his own road to salvation.'[9]

Why was Frederick's reaction so different from that of Maria Theresa? Can we find the answer to this simply in the political context of his kingdom? His territories were certainly, from 1740 until at least the mid 1760s, being continually expanded, not only by warfare but also by a continuous process of exchange and negotiation aimed at bringing together widely scattered territories in as united a territorial bloc as possible. Frederick was also recruiting skilled labour from all over Europe to aid the economic and industrial development of Prussia. To enforce religious uniformity in all these circumstances would have been very difficult.

But arguments for toleration based on its economic utility or political convenience, strongly though they were made, are not enough to explain differences in attitudes between rulers on this issue. The argument for toleration on economic grounds seemed overwhelming to Joseph II, and was undoubtedly accepted by Frederick the Great; it did not impress Maria Theresa enough for her to cease large-scale state persecution of Protestants residing in Bohemia and in Hungary. Nor is it other than misleading to draw distinctions between Catholic and Protestant rulers on this issue. If Maria Theresa persecuted non-Catholics, non-Protestants certainly did not gain full equality of status and rights (though they were usually less dramatically mis-treated), in any majority Protestant state, apart from the British North American colonies, which had no established church, and possibly in the Netherlands. Everywhere, Jews laboured under more disadvantages than did their Christian neighbours of any denomination. In fact, Frederick's view in Prussia that all sects would be tolerated, as long as they made no special claims, was highly unusual in the eighteenth century. It pointed the way in which Frederick's monarchy showed a more rapid evolution away from traditional models than any other, with the possible exception of the British. In religious terms, this meant that Frederick explored, perhaps more thoroughly than any other ruler, the freedoms conferred by the ending of interstate confessional warfare at the end of the seventeenth century.

[9] Quoted in H.W. Koch, *A History of Prussia* (London, 1978), 41.

The religious denominations themselves also had to explore this new situation. After 1648, it was not only international conflict over religion that began to die down; so did, though with some important exceptions, internecine conflict between the sects. Over a hundred years of conflict since Luther, had demonstrated to many the impossibility of convincing others of religious truths either by appeals to the authority of the churches, or to revelation, supernatural knowledge of things spiritual which could only be told to men by God through specially chosen human channels such as the prophets. Many in all religious denominations became anxious to construct a version of their faith, which could be apprehended by human *reason*, which would thus be accessible to all men alike, and should thus convince without the need to resort to force. It is no accident that in 1695, John Locke should publish a book, significantly entitled *The Reasonableness of Christianity*.

Behind the push to construct a 'reasonable' Christianity lay the hideous memory of sectarian strife, often accompanied by threat of social revolution, which had been so prevalent in the seventeenth century. It was also motivated by continuous, sporadic outbursts of religious hostilities within states, even in the eighteenth century itself. Protestants in Lithuania were persecuted by their Polish rulers in the 1720s. Protestants in Hungary and Bohemia were harried. There were renewed outbursts against Protestants in France from the 1740s at least until the famous Calas and Sirvin cases of the mid 1760s. The drive to construct a 'reasonable' version of Christianity was fuelled by those outbursts as much as by the memories of the preceding century.[10]

But 'reasonable Christianity' also brought along new problems of its own. If Christianity was to be recast in a form which any rational person could accept, what happened to the status of the Bible, so full of the irrational and of the personal testimony of the prophets and apostles, who had certainly not received the revelation of 'a new heaven and a new earth' through rationality? What happened to apparently irrational occurrences, such as the miracles performed by Christ which overturned the laws of nature? Thus a questioning of the status and authority of the Bible was to be a major – if unintended – by-product of the attempt to establish 'reasonable' Christianity.

The attempt to downplay revelation in favour of reason also had other consequences. Revelation was, by definition, that which Christianity did not share with other faiths. As the century progressed, and knowledge of other religions grew, it was increasingly and unforgettably realised that much of what had been seen as specific to the Christian religion had in fact

[10] D. Bien, *The Calas Affair; Reason, Tolerance and Heresy in Eighteenth-Century Toulouse* (Princeton, 1960).

many analogues in other faiths. Legends of a great flood, for example, appeared in many oriental cultures without historical links to Judaism or Christianity.[11] Increasing interest in other religions, was also to lead to the study of religion as a human creation, rather than a revelation by the Divine of itself. This new focus is revealed, for example, in David Hume's 1757 *Natural History of Religion*, and in the growing interest throughout the century in what we would now call the field of 'comparative religion'. Voltaire's theologian was not a unique figure in the Enlightenment; nor was his increasing uncertainty surrounding the status of Christian belief in relation to that of other religions.

If the new field of the study of comparative religion was unsettling, science itself sent ambiguous messages into the religious thinking of the Enlightenment. For centuries it had been customary to point to nature and to cosmology as evidence of God's power and benevolence. The earth had been created, it was argued, as a benevolently ordered habitat for man, who had the right to control and exploit other created beings in his own interest.[12] Astronomical work in the sixteenth century by Copernicus and Kepler, however, had demonstrated that far from being the stable centre of the cosmos, planet earth revolved around a sun and was itself only one of many planetary systems.

In 1687, Isaac Newton (1642–1727) published his *Mathematical Principles of Natural Philosophy*. In spite of its difficult mathematics, this work had tremendous impact throughout the Enlightenment, as it seemed to provide a basis for answering the question of what *sort* of interest God actually displayed in his creation. Did he intervene daily in the lives of his chosen, as the Old Testament seemed to imply? Or was his interest far more remote, or non-existent? Newton himself portrayed an ordered cosmos subject to mathematical laws, not only originally set in motion by its creator, but also requiring considerable intervention from him to correct irregularities and supply energy. The cosmos, as Newton originally envisaged it, could be seen as a vast proof of both God's existence, and of his continuing concern at least for his physical creation, if not in the day-to-day doings of men.

Many of Newton's popularisers, such as Voltaire himself, whose work reached an audience far larger than did Newton's original text, interpreted the *Mathematical Principles* as showing God's *distance* from his creation. Newton's work thus was used in ways far removed from his original intentions, to support those who the century called Deists, who

---

[11] Hans Frei, *The Eclipse of Biblical Narrative* (New Haven, 1977); P.J. Marshall, *The British Discovery of Hinduism in the Eighteenth Century* (Cambridge, 1970); G.R. Cragg, *Reason and Authority in Eighteenth-Century England* (Cambridge, 1964).

[12] K. Thomas, *Man and the Natural World* (London, 1983).

believed in God only as the creator of the universe, a Being thus virtually equivalent to the laws of nature itself. Such a God displayed no interest in the moral choices of men, but existed only as a First Cause.[13] Meanwhile, the Scots historian and philosopher David Hume pointed out that the existence of the order of nature, or of the laws of the cosmos did not necessarily betray anything about the nature of its creator, or indeed that there had been a creator at all. However, this eminently logical conclusion was read by relatively few people. While popularisations of Newton's work received a much larger audience throughout Europe and the Americas, and undoubtedly provided fruitful ammunition for doubters and Deists, most eighteenth-century people still believed in the idea of the earth and the cosmos as created by a benevolent God as a suitable habitat for man. Paradoxically, as the century drew to a close, and well into the next, a favourite argument for the existence of God, especially in Protestant countries, continued to be the 'order and contrivance' of nature. In this, as in much else, science sent contradictory messages into Enlightenment religious development.

Nor was this confusion unique to this particular area of the religious thought of the Enlightenment. Older, orthodox beliefs, and Enlightenment speculation sat uneasily side by side in the minds of many. Throughout the century, while *philosophes* preached the natural goodness and perfectability of man, orthodox theologians continued to emphasise his innate sinfulness, due to the sin of Adam, and to thunder about the Divine retribution which would surely follow sinners after death.[14] The problem raised here was a deeper one than that of maintaining clarity in the mind of the average believer. It returned to a central tenet of the Christian religion, the divine nature of Christ, and the necessity for his sacrifice on the Cross to redeem man from the sinful condition into which Adam's disobedience had thrown him. If man was not in fact innately sinful, what need to believe in Christ?

At the same time, belief in Christ's divinity was coming under attack from another quarter. Proof of his divinity was held to be the miracles which Christ performed, and which were attested to in the Gospels. Such miracles, such as the rising of Lazarus from the dead, or the changing of water into wine at the wedding at Cana, or the very Resurrection itself, all involved an overthrow of the laws of nature, those very laws of nature which many in the Enlightenment were so eager totally to identify with God. In 1748, David Hume's *Essay on Miracles*, published six years after

---

[13] P. Gay, *Deism: An Anthology* (Princeton, 1968).
[14] John McManners, *Death and the Enlightenment: Changing Attitudes to Death among Christians and Unbelievers in Eighteenth-Century France* (Oxford, 1981); C. McDonnell and B. Long, *Heaven: A History* (New Haven, 1988).

Dublin audiences flocked to the first performance of Handel's *Messiah* which celebrated the miraculous birth and resurrection of Christ, laid much of the ground-work for subsequent controversy, together with Voltaire's 1765 *Questions sur les Miracles*. A Newtonian view of the laws of nature brought into doubt the *likelihood* of miracles actually occurring. Hume also pointed out that the 'evidence' for the miracles of Christ having occurred, lay with the allegedly eyewitness accounts in the Gospels and that eyewitness accounts were often the least reliable of all forms of evidence. How could the reliability of the Gospel witnesses be assessed, he asked, if there are no contemporary analogues to the events they relate? Certainly there was no contemporary analogue for the most important miracle of all, the Resurrection. Hume also pointed out that while human testimony might be a *necessary* part of establishing the credibility of miracles (otherwise we would not even know of their existence), human eyewitness testimony was not sufficient to lend credibility to accounts of events that were contradicted both by the laws of nature, and by present day human experience.

Debates on the nature of historical knowledge, and its relationship to religion also entered the fray. German *philosophes* such as Gotthold Ephraim Lessing (1729–81) and most famously, Johann Gottlieb Fichte (1762–1814) pointed out that historical study could only show 'what happened' not the ethical meaning, or rational status of events. Because of this, they argued, the historical data in the New Testament were insufficient to establish its status as revelation. At the same time, historians in the eighteenth century increasingly abandoned the medieval and Renaissance view of history as by definition the story of the working out of divine intentions in the 'theatre of the world' inhabited by sinful humans. They came much closer to the view of history espoused by the Neapolitan historian Giambattista Vico (1668–1744) that history should be seen as the story of man's *own* capacity for progress. Edward Gibbon (1737–94) for example, was to provide in his famous *Decline and Fall of the Roman Empire* (1776, Chapter 15), an account of the rise of early Christianity as a purely *human* organisation, whose development could be understood in exactly the same terms as those of the Roman Empire itself.

Miracles thus became an increasing target for anti-religious thinkers like d'Holbach. The miracle stories were easily attacked as belonging to a long line of priestly confidence tricks on an ignorant and credulous people. For those influenced by the work of Newton, or who wished to construct a 'reasonable' religion, miracles were also a problem: Why should God have wished to disrupt his own natural and rational laws? None of this made the status of central Christian beliefs any more secure among those of the educated classes who were aware of these debates, though they probably had little impact on the mass of ordinary believers, particularly in Catholic countries; nor was it the intention of the *philosophes* to destroy what they saw as the simple (and socially necessary) faith of their social inferiors, by diffusing their own rational enquiries too far down the social scale.

Nor was all Enlightenment questioning of religious teaching based on simple logical enquiry. At times, events focussed minds on particular issues which had always been problematical in Christian teaching. One such 'focussing moment' occurred in 1755, when an earthquake, followed by a tidal wave, killed more than 10,000 people in the city of Lisbon and reduced most of the city to ruins. How, asked Voltaire and many others, could this event be reconciled with a conception of God as a loving or omnipotent creator? How could God have permitted such a misfortune to occur to so many people? The problem of the existence of evil was hardly new in the eighteenth century. But what the Lisbon earthquake did was to focus minds on the discrepancy between the existence of evil and of unmerited misfortune, and the increasing optimism taught by many Enlightenment thinkers. This 'optimism' had become so prevalent that the philosopher Leibnitz had coined the new term, 'theodicy', to describe the repeated attempts to 'solve' the problem of evil, or provide an explanation of its existence consistent with the possibility of a 'reasonable' religion and of a benevolent and omnipotent creator. By 1759, Voltaire, in his significantly entitled *Candide or Optimism*, was able mercilessly to satirise Leibnitz in his character of Dr Pangloss, who believes that this is the 'best of all possible worlds'.[15] Such a change from optimism could only destabilise Christian belief even further.

There were many different responses to these problems. One way out was Deism, with its total hostility to revelation. Another was to reject the attempt to make Christianity 'reasonable', and return to a view of religion which emphasised faith, trust in revelation, and personal witness to religious experience. In this way came much impetus for the new 'enthusiastic' religious sects, such as Methodism, which broke away from Anglicanism in England and the religious revival known as the 'Great Awakening' in the North American British colonies. Much the same original impulse lay behind the movement known as Pietism in North Germany.[16]

In looking at Pietism, we are looking at the way in which religious issues could move far beyond the polite discussions of elites, and have dramatic

[15] Francis-Marie Arouet de Voltaire, *Candide ou l'Optimisme* (Paris, 1759).
[16] The following discussion of Pietism owes much to M. Fulbrooke, *Piety and Politics: Religion and the Rise of Absolutism in England, Württemburg and Prussia* (Cambridge, 1983).

effects on society and government. Pietism was a movement of religious revival which swept through the Protestant states of Germany in the aftermath of the Thirty Years' War, which Pietists saw as a terrible punishment for sin inflicted on Germany by God. Its founders emphasised an idea of personal religious experience far removed from contemporary attempts to create a 'reasonable Christianity'. The early Pietists were concerned to work within the Lutheran church for its reform. For them, the struggles over religion since the early sixteenth century had resulted in Lutheranism paying too much attention to the reform of the church, and too little to the issue of how the church might reform the world. While many German princes viewed the movement with hostility because of its capacity to create religious disturbance in society, and to upset their *modus vivendi* with the Lutheran church, the ruler of Prussia, Frederick William I (1688–1740), welcomed the movement with open arms. The Prussian Elector saw how to use Pietism's enthusiasm for the reform of the world, which was chanelled in Prussia into dedication to serving the poor and serving the state. In Prussia at least, Pietism was not merely a vehicle for ecstatic religious witness and the awaiting of the Second Coming of Christ, but an active social and political force. Frederick William used Pietism to drive a wedge into the formerly strong links binding the Lutheran church in Prussia to the Estates, or representative bodies of the nobility, many of which were opposed to his plans for centralisation and reform. The Elector handed over the control of education and of other institutions formerly dominated by orthodox Lutherans to known Pietists. Pietism, as Fulbrooke has argued, thus became a powerful force enhancing the power of the ruler over the social elites and the Lutheran church, providing a powerful force for cultural unity in Prussia's divided lands. The spread of Pietism's ideas of service to others and to the state, was crucial to the conversion of the Prussian nobility into a court-orientated service bureaucracy, without which Prussian absolutism could not have emerged or functioned.

This also means that even for a new and active sect such as the Pietists, the impact of their religious beliefs cannot be read off from their dogma alone, but was altered by the social and political context in which they operated. What was an ecstatic, emotional, socially disruptive, sect in Württemburg, was an organised force in the service of the state in Prussia.

It is also important to note that in the Enlightenment almost all major faiths developed internally generated reforming movements. Where Lutheranism had Pietism, Catholicism had Jansenism, and Anglicanism had Methodism. Just as the Elector Frederick William used Pietism to further his own reform plans, so did the Grand-Duke Peter Leopold of Tuscany use the Jansenist faction to further his own plans for church reform, despite the opposition of much of the Catholic hierarchy. In Austria too, Jansenism was a powerful factor behind demands to reform. In spite of the fact that in many of the states, such as France, Jansenism was interpreted as a threat to monarchal powers, rather than its support, all this shows nonetheless, how aware were Enlightenment rulers of the social function of religion. It is arguable that the success of Prussian Pietism in the years before 1740 in bolstering the power of the ruler, was what made it possible for Frederick the Great to have enough power to enforce his policy of tolerance after 1740.

Additional tensions were present in many Catholic states, where the ruler's allegiance to the church, and their reliance on its ritual to legitimise their authority as rulers, did not prevent renewed conflict between monarchy and the church hierarchy. In the Austrian lands too, it was strongly believed, especially by Joseph II, that control of education should be transferred from the Catholic church to the state; and that the allegiance of his subjects to their duties could be better inculcated by the teaching of a 'rational' Christianity. All sought for more independence from Rome and increasing control over religious observance, and church appointments in their own lands. The expulsion of the Jesuit order, sworn to uphold Papal power, from all Catholic countries between the 1759 and 1771 is only the most dramatic example of this tension. Spurred on too, especially in the Italian states and in Josephian Austria, by economic advisors who believed that the land market was underdeveloped and agricultural productivity held back by the Church's role as predominant landlord, and that monastic orders were detaining many potential recruits to the labour force and the army, many Catholic monarchs, such as Joseph II and Charles III of Spain, launched attacks on the church.

The picture which emerges of religion in the Enlightenment is thus complex. In terms of belief, traditional theology competed with new religious sects such as Pietism, and more fundamentally with religious enquiries such as Deism, which seemed bent on nothing so much as removing religion from religious belief. Attempts to construct a 'reasonable' or 'rational' Christianity caused as many problems as they solved. Some historians have argued, and Hegel would probably have agreed, that Deists and 'reasonable' Christians alike ran the risk of erecting human reason itself as the focus of a new religion, while social movements such as the Masonic Lodges could easily be seen as the outward sign of new, secular, substitute cults, and were so especially in Catholic countries.[17]

Religious change and debate also had profound consequences in the

[17] See the argument of Carl Becker, *The Heavenly City of the Eighteenth-Century Philosophers* (New Haven, 1932).

political sphere. It is a truism that the central metaphor of political thought in the seventeenth century was religious, whereas the eighteenth century sees the slow breakdown of the idea that political and religious communities must be co-terminous. This was the logic involved in the debate on religious toleration which took place all over Europe, and which involved those rulers and communities which supported it in a conscious effort to change the basis of legitimate power. This is the major reason why the implementation of freely debated ideas of religious toleration, so obvious to us, took such a long time, and involved such hard debate in the eighteenth century. For those rulers who implemented toleration would have to base their legitimation on something other than religious sanction. Debating toleration was thus ultimately debating the nature of kingship itself (see chapter 7). The issue was thus an intrinsic part of what some historians have described as the 'desacralisation' of kingship in this period. In this sense, as in others, Hegel was surely right to see Enlightenment as a continuation of the Reformation. Whether it also thereby opened the gates to revolution is another matter, to be discussed in chapter 8.

4   Science and the Enlightenment: God's order and man's understanding

The Creator doubtless did not bestow so much curiosity and exquisite workmanship and skill upon his creatures, to be looked upon with a careless or incurious eye, especially to have them slighted or condemned; but to be admired by the rational part of the world, to magnify his own power, wisdom and goodness throughout all the world, and the ages thereof ... my text commends God's works, not only for being great, but also approves of those curious and ingenious enquirers, that seek them out, or pry into them. And the more we pry into and discover of them, the greater and more glorious we find them to be, the more worthy of, and the more expressly to proclaim their great Creator.

The first man I saw was of a meagre aspect, with sooty hands and face, his hair and beard long, ragged and singed in several places. His clothes, shirt, and skin were all of the same colour. He had been eight years upon a project for extracting sunbeams out of cucumbers, which were to be put into vials heremetically sealed, and let out to warm the air in raw inclement summers. He told me, he did not doubt in eight years more, that he should be able to supply the Governor's gardens with sunshine at a reasonable rate; but he complained that his stock was low, and entreated me to give him something as an encouragement to ingenuity, especially since this had been a very dear season for cucumbers. I made him a small present, for my Lord had furnished me with money on purpose, because he knew their practice of begging from all who go to see them.[1]

Science is today probably the most powerful force in twentieth-century culture. It determines our potential for technological control of the environment, many of our cultural and intellectual assumptions, and our economic, technological and even agricultural base. In the twentieth century almost all science receives some form of public funding, and scientific practices and assumptions have also heavily influenced much current thinking about the way governments should be run. None of this

---

[1] William Derham, *Physico-Theology: or, a Demonstration of the Being and Attributes of God, from His Works of Creation* (2 vols., London 1798) II, 394, first published, 1713; Jonathan Swift, *Gulliver's Travels* (1726) London, 1967), 223–4 (A Voyage to Laputa, part III, section 5).

was the case in the eighteenth century. The intellectual status of science was contested, its institutional organisations often weak, and certainly thin on the ground, and the nature of its relations with the economy and with government often tenuous. No institution of science was a major employer of labour, and educational structures in most countries paid little attention to disseminating scientific knowledge. Only a few men could support themselves by full-time work in science.

Nonetheless, science in this period is still an important topic, and not only because of its forerunner status to the expansion of science in subsequent centuries. Precisely because science *was* an insecure form of knowledge in the eighteenth century, it had to confront many crucial questions in the way that the established science of today, which can concentrate on problem solving *within* a clearly delineated intellectual area, often does not. Eighteenth-century science had to grapple with such larger issues as the relationship of man to nature, the very possibility of knowledge of the external world, and of the best way to organise such knowledge. Science also acted as the link between many apparently diverse areas of Enlightenment thought. As we have seen, it was also deeply implicated in contemporary religious development (chapter 3). 'Nature', the very subject matter of science, has also been described by many as an 'ethical norm' in the Enlightenment. What was 'natural' must be 'good'. Others have argued that science embodied the central Enlightenment value of 'reason' or 'rationality'. By 'rationality' was usually meant objective thinking, without passion, prejudice or superstition, and without reference to non-verifiable statements such as those of religious revelation. More recently, the French philosopher Michel Foucault, put forward the controversial but influential view that the development of Enlightenment science was paradigmatic of deep changes in the structures of *all* knowledge in this period.[2] Thus, for some historians science is the cultural category of the Enlightenment, rather than that of religion which seems so central to Hegel.

There thus seems to be ample reason to devote attention to science in the Enlightenment. But a word of warning is necessary. In using this word 'science' at all, we are in fact committing the sin of anachronism. The words 'science' and 'scientist' were not invented until the 1830s in England. Before that 'natural philosophy' was probably the term most in use. In French *'science'* like the German *Wissenschaft*, meant 'knowledge'

---

[2] A.O. Lovejoy, 'Nature as an Aesthetic Norm', in *Essays in the History of Ideas* (New York, 1960), 69–77. Michel Foucault, *The Order of Things: An Archaeology of the Human Sciences* (New York, 1973). According to Foucault, taxonomy served during this period not only as the dominant impulse for the pursuit of natural history, but as the organising principle for *all* intellectual activity.

or 'knowing', and was not necessarily connected with knowledge of nature. The term *'scientifique'* to label specifically those involved in such investigation was a coinage of the late nineteenth century.[3] Thus, in two major languages there was no word specifically to describe enquiry into nature, or its practitioners. This should alert us to the extent to which 'science' was not yet separated out from other intellectual areas, nor were its practitioners readily distinguished from practitioners of other forms of intellectual enquiry. Enlightenment normality was typified by Voltaire, who worked on a popularisation of Newtonian mathematical physics, while also producing plays, poems, short stories, and political criticism; or by Diderot, whose speculations on the organisation of nature, and the nature of human perception occurred in the midst of other enquiries and discussions, such as those contained in *Rameau's Nephew* or on colonialism in his *Supplément au Voyage de Bougainville*.

The linguistic point also reveals the extent to which 'science' was not yet a defined body of knowledge, not yet a 'discipline', a body of knowledge separate from other bodies of knowledge, with its own subject matter, let alone divided into sub-disciplines such as 'physiology' or 'geology'. The study of what we now call 'science' still took place in the eighteenth century within other disciplines, linked together under the heading of 'natural philosophy'. In turn, as a recent historian has noted 'the whole point of "natural philosophy" was to look at nature and the world as created by God, and thus as capable of being understood as embodying God's powers and purposes'.[4]

This statement is particularly true for the 'natural philosophy' practised in the English-speaking Enlightenment, but it was also a strong factor in much of the natural philosophy undertaken in continental Europe. In an age much concerned with the construction of a 'reasonable Christianity' (chapter 3) which could offer information about God and his purposes independent of 'irrational' sources such as faith and revelation, science with its appeal to the evidence of the senses, was an essential reference in theological debate. For example, the title of John Ray's 1692 *The Wisdom of God Manifested in the Works of The Creation*, could stand for many others of the time. The natural order was also implicated in the arguments of those Deists who thought of God as little more than the original force behind the laws of nature, to the extent that the Deity and the laws of nature often seemed little more than synonyms.

---

[3] Sydney Ross, '"Scientist": The Story of a Word', *Annals of Science*, 18 (1962), 65–86; Raymond Williams, *Keywords: A Vocabulary of Culture and Society* (London, 1976), s.v. 'science'.

[4] A. Cunningham and P. Williams, 'De-centring the Big Picture', *British Journal for the History of Science*, 26 (1993), 407–32.

'Natural philosophy' thus functioned within this wider framework to a greater or lesser extent, in most European states. This often made it nearly impossible to establish where 'natural philosophy' ended, and where theology, 'the Queen of the sciences' began. It was not easy for the study of nature to become a separate intellectual discipline, with a separate body of practitioners. The link between natural philosophy and theology was tightened by the fact that much natural philosophy, particularly in Protestant states, was done by members of the clergy. Leisure, education and a rural vicarage were the source of much observational science.

The quest for a 'reasonable Christianity' thus did throw natural philosophy into a place of increasing importance in the Enlightenment. But, 'Nature' also started to assume importance in a rather different sense. For 'natural philosophy', 'nature' was seen as an expression of God's ordering hand and was, therefore, largely represented, despite considerable evidence to the contrary, as ordered, as obeying 'laws' and as providing a benevolent habitat for man, who was thus enabled by God to carry out His purposes. 'Nature', however, also had other important meanings in the Enlightenment, many of which were extensions and secularisations of the ideas behind 'natural philosophy'. The 'natural' was seen as the 'good', meaning original, authentic, simple, uncorrupted, and, by extension, in the works of Rousseau and others, as a state opposed to 'civilisation' with all its artificiality and corruption (chapter 6). Thus 'nature' became a description of a moral ideal as well as of a scientifically discernible order, and was thus seen as something which could reside in the hearts of men, as much as being an external order visible and tangible and measurable to natural philosophers. The meaning of 'nature' was thus notoriously imprecise. It, and the search for 'reasonable Christianity' together heightened the importance of enquiry into 'nature' in Enlightenment thinking. They certainly did not provide a secure methodology for the actual conduct of science.

But if 'nature' was to function either as an ethical norm or as a Christian image, natural philosophy had to be underpinned by ideas about how it was possible to know 'nature' at all. Older intellectual traditions which denigrated knowledge of the external world still had considerable force in this period, traditions which greatly pre-dated the popular Enlightenment idea that it was not only possible but proper to deduce the existence and nature of the creator from that of his creation. Among ordinary people, science was also seen as ridiculous or even useless. In 1740, for example, the Swedish naturalist Charles Linnaeus, whose nomenclature systems still survive in botany, felt impelled to answer critics who questioned the very purpose of science. He wrote one question is always asked, one objection always made to those who are curious about nature, when ill-educated people (*le vulgaire*) see natural philosophers examining the products of nature. They ask, often with mocking laughter, 'What's the use of it' ... Such people think that natural philosophy is only about the gratification of curiosity, only an amusement to pass the time for lazy and thoughtless people.[5]

Linnaeus, like Swift's depiction of Laputa, gives a picture of the serious natural philosopher not only as besieged by the ridicule and incomprehension of the uneducated, but also by a strong prejudice *against* the gratification of intellectual curiosity. In the middle ages and the Renaissance, curiosity had a bad name, both as a form of lust and as the impulse which had resulted in the expulsion of Adam and Eve from Paradise. This was a point of view which the continuous publication of earlier theological writings kept firmly alive. Even by 1762, Rousseau was still having to argue in his influential educational text, *Emile*, that curiosity was a virtue which could bring benefits by enhancing knowledge.[6]

Even sections of society which had jettisoned moral qualms over curiosity about the created world, faced other problems concerning the status of scientific knowledge. How, philosophers asked, could men ever know the external world of nature, or, knowing it, how could they be certain that their knowledge *was* accurate? How was it possible to reduce the dazzling succession of events and entities in nature to general laws which might be predictive? Many argued, as did the Neopolitan historian Giambattista Vico (1688–1744) in his aptly named *Scienza Nuova* (1725), that 'natural philosophy' could never really be a secure form of knowledge. Vico argued that if one is seeking universal and eternal principles in a field of knowledge, principles that make it proper to call it a 'science', one must look to things of *human* creation, such as human history and human institutions. Physical 'science', for example deals with entities, of which we can never have direct experience, and which are thus completely foreign to us. We can only make up theories which are more or less *probable* about physical objects. But we can have an intuitive *certainty* in our understanding of the needs and desires that unite the human race across the ages, and which can be checked against common human experience. Vico's arguments were to be echoed by many others down the century, and it remained a commonplace that historical and literary

[5] B. Jasmin and Camille Limoges (eds.), C. Linné, 'A Quoi-Sert-il' in *L'Equilibre de la Nature* (Paris, 1972), 145–6.

[6] J. Céard (ed.), *La curiosité à la Rennaissance* (Paris, 1986); [M. Landois], 'Curieux'; [Chevalier de Jaucourt], 'Curiosité', in D'Alembert and Diderot (eds.), *Encyclopédie* (Paris, 1754), 577–8; Jacques-Bénigne Bossuet, *Traîté de la concupiscence* (1731) eds. C. Urbain and E. Lenesque (Paris, 1930), esp. chapter 8. J.J. Rousseau, *Emile ou de l'éducation* (1762) ed. F. and P. Richard (Paris, 1964), 185, 271.

3 This is the title page of Thomas Burnett's 1684 *Sacred Theory of the Earth*, one of the most influential early Enlightenment statements of the confluence between the history of Nature and the events of Biblical narrative. Christ stands astride the seven phases of the history of nature, including the creation, the Great Flood in the third phase, and the end of the world in fire (fifth phase).

judgements, for Vico's reasons, were far more stable than knowledge of nature, and thus represented a superior kind of intellectual outcome.

Those Enlightenment thinkers who did try to find a basis for knowledge of the external world, such John Locke or Etienne Condillac (1715–80), broke away from previous thinking and emphasised the role of sense impressions of the external world in the formation of abstract concepts. A consequence of this belief was that man could know only appearances, not the real essences of external things:

> Ideas in no way allow us to know beings as they actually are; they merely depict them in terms of their relationship with us, and this alone is enough to prove the vanity of the efforts of those philosophers who pretend to penetrate into the nature of things.[7]

Because of the way in which our ideas of the external world were formed, natural philosophy, in other words, could never explain 'first principles', the causes of causes. And so, while many continued to accept that natural philosophy and theology should operate co-operatively, philosophy in practice laid more emphasis on the constraints on the possibility of human beings gaining any deep knowledge of the natural order. Paradoxically, this was to be a first step along the road to science becoming an entirely distinct form of intellectual endeavour, of its gradual separation from the 'first order' questions dominant in theology, the 'Queen of Sciences'.

But if science could not peer into the heart of things, could it at least construct a picture of the external world which would be coherent and orderly and law governed – a picture which might not be deeply 'true', but could at least be self-consistent? Here too, however, the philosophers did not make things easy for those interested in the natural world. Statements that one thing causes another are clearly highly important in 'natural philosophy'. Chemists, for example, like to be able to say that the presence of certain chemicals *causes* a certain reaction. But even the validity of such causal statements were challenged. The Scots philosopher David Hume contested the belief held by Descartes – and, for different reasons, by later thinkers such as Locke and Condillac – that there was an easy way of guaranteeing the validity of any transition from the fragmentary and transient world our sense impressions reveal to us to the orderly and 'lawful' world described especially in the physical sciences. Hume explains the fact that human beings do seem routinely able to make this transition, by reference to what he calls 'custom', socially agreed ways which act as facilitators for humans to make the leap from the world of sense impressions to the ordered depiction of the natural world which they portray as the 'natural order'. As Hume wrote:

[7] Etienne Bonnot de Condillac, *Traîté des Sensations* (Paris, 1754).

I may venture to affirm of mankind, that they are nothing but a bundle or collection of different perceptions, which succeed each other with an inconceivable rapidity, in a perpetual flux and movement.[8]

Because of this the causal claims so central to some branches of natural philosophy, particularly in the cosmological and physical sciences, could not be given absolute legitimation, once science shifted from *describing* a divinely instituted natural order, to enquiring into its causal relations. While scientific accounts of causal relationships could claim to be more or less self-consistent, their truth-value had to remain debatable. Hume argued that the only thing which impels us to connect events in terms of causation is previous experiences of similar sequences. Our *habit* is to reason causally; but nothing guarantees that causal reasoning produces truth, rather than consistency with appearances; and nothing guarantees that these appearances will always appear in the same sequence. That the sun has risen for millions of days before today does not guarantee that the sun will rise tomorrow.

It is difficult to reconcile these ideas, which had a great impact on European philosophers such as Immanuel Kant, with the presupposition central to theology, that nature as God's creation really could be said to be actually existing 'out there', reflecting the order, contrivance and plenitude of the Divine mind itself, and that that natural order would gradually become more and more accessible to human beings. In Hume's account, there was no obstacle to this actually being the case; but it also seemed that a huge number of obstacles inherent in man's own perceptions had been created to men ever being able to perceive the natural order in a way they could guarantee was 'true' rather than 'probable'. Thus, it seemed unlikely that knowledge of God, or 'reasonable Christianity' could be supported by the findings of 'natural philosophy'. Because of this, Hume also argued that it was impossible to reason from the character of the natural order, as constructed by human natural philosophers, to the character of the Deity. The creator could not be presumed from His creation.

Thus, 'natural philosophy' operated in an increasingly strained relationship with philosophical enquiry which undercut its capacity to carry out the objectives of theology. This did not prevent natural philosophy, with all its theological presuppositions, from being enthusiastically endorsed in actual practice, particularly in English-speaking and Prot-

---

[8] David Hume, *A Treatise of Human Nature* (1739) Book I, IV, chapter VI. This section also owes much to Ernest Gellner, *Reason and Culture: The Historic Role of Rationality and Rationalism* (Oxford, 1992), esp. 20–3. It should be noted that Kant emphasises that we do need to act *as if* causality is real, otherwise we have no way of describing location, size, or stability.

estant countries. But it does mean that we cannot say that the Enlightenment unanimously endorsed scientific enquiry as the best or most
'rational' form of knowledge. There were severe and persistent doubts
about its standing and 'truth value', as well as its utility and stability in
comparison to the historical and literary, let alone theological 'sciences'.

Yet, enquiry into nature did develop in this period, and did end the
century with a higher status than at the beginning, though never
approaching the dominant place in culture which it has assumed in our
own times. Partly, this was because the doubts expressed by even well-
known writers like Hume, who was better known in his own day as an
historian, seem to have had little impact on the actual practice of science,
or on the cultural importance of natural theology in English-speaking
countries. The reason for this might be that philosophers almost always
began their questioning of science not from the actual *practice* or utility of
science, but from the predicament of an individual 'observer' facing
'nature'. Men like Hume and Kant, in spite of the importance of their
legacy, did not address the questions of how and why science *can* operate
as an activity pursued in common by human beings in a social setting. In
this they reflected the comparative social and institutional weaknesses of
science in the world around them, as well as reflecting the common
emphasis placed by Enlightenment philosophy on an ideal, solitary,
representative individual as encapsulating truth.

It is now time to look at what 'science' was actually doing in the
Enlightenment.[9] At many points, we can see that natural philosophy was
gradually separating itself from theological ends. This is one interpretation of the work of the century's most famous scientific figure, Isaac
Newton (1643–1727). It is certainly possible to argue that the Enlightenment opens not only with John Locke's attempts to understand the
human mind and human society, but also with Newton's attempts in his
1687 *Mathematical Principles of Natural Philosophy (Philosophiae Naturalis Principia Mathematica)* to produce mathematical descriptions of the
cosmic order, the motions of planets, the famous law of universal
gravitation, and the idea of planetary space as infinite. Newton's achieve-

---

[9] It is impossible in a single chapter to present the entire range of scientific activity in the
Enlightenment and this chapter concentrates on two areas: Newtonian cosmology and
natural history. Information on other important fields of science can be found in, e.g.,
G.S. Rousseau and R.S. Porter (eds.), *The Ferment of Knowledge: Studies in the
Historiography of Eighteenth-Century Science* (Cambridge, 1980); R. Porter, *The Making
of Geology: Earth Science in Britain, 1660–1815* (Cambridge, 1979); L.J. Jordanova and
R. Porter (eds.), *Images of the Earth: Essays in the History of the Environmental Sciences*
(Chalfont St Giles, 1978); J. Roger, *Les sciences de la vie dans la penseé française au dix-
huitième siècle* (Paris, 1963); J. Heilbron, *Electricity in the Seventeenth and Eighteenth
Centuries: A Study of Early Modern Physics* (Berkeley, 1979); F.L. Holmes, *Lavoisier
and the Chemistry of Life: An Exploration of Scientific Creativity* (Madison, WI., 1985).

ments were transmitted down the century by a host of popularisers in most European countries, which, as we have seen, even included Voltaire, and which played into a growing market for popular science. Each populariser introduced his own distortions as they produced verbal equivalents to what were complex and demanding mathematical expressions.[10] Most contrived to produce an idea that Newton had described the whole of the created universe and had described that order as a self-regulating balanced system of lawful movement. In many of these popular accounts, it might appear that whatever the theoretical objections to the possibility of our knowledge of the external world might be, at least physical laws of motion could be completely described by self-consistent mathematical systems.

Newton's views were in fact much more complex. He stated that while it was possible to describe the cosmos mathematically, it was not possible to use mathematics to answer 'first-order' questions as to *how* the cosmos was *kept* in being and in motion. Newton himself also denied that his laws *did* describe a self-generating, self-regulating universe. As he said, motion 'is much more apt to be lost than got, it is always upon the decay'. Energy, he thought, could only be restored to the cosmic system by the direct, periodic intervention of its creator. Newton's ideas seemed to have shown the necessity of some First Cause to keep the cosmos functioning; but in spite of the statements of some of the popularisers, it provided no guarantee that that First Cause in any way resembled the God of the Old or New Testaments, or that there was any scientific grounding for the tenets of Christianity.[11]

Newton's impact was mixed. In the 1690s, the theologian, Richard Bently preached sermons which enlisted Newton in defence of religion. By 1734, the divine and philosopher, George Berkeley (1685–1753) saw Newtonianism as conducive to heresy and atheism. There was even disagreement as to how Newton had actually achieved his results. D'Alembert, in his 1751 Introduction to the *Encyclopédie*, invoked Newton to show the supremacy of mathematical analysis in science, while others saw Newton's work as a triumph of pure observation. Others hoped that Newton's prestige could legitimate a 'science of man' that would be as lawful as his natural philosophy. Even as late as 1802, the French Utopian thinker Claude-Henri St-Simon (1760–1825), whom many have seen as one of the grandfathers of Socialism, proposed a social

[10] Popularisations include such European best-sellers as Francesco Algarotti, *Il Newtonismo per le Dame* (1737), and for children, John Newberry, *Tom Telescope's Philosophy of Tops and Balls* (London, 1761).

[11] The literature on Newton is vast. I.B. Cohen, *The Newtonian Revolution* (Cambridge, 1980) is probably the most accessible and comprehensive recent account.

PRINCIPES
MATHÉMATIQUES

DE LA

PHILOSOPHIE NATURELLE,

Par feue Madame la Marquise DU CHASTELLET.

TOME PREMIER.

A PARIS,

Chez
{
DESAINT & SAILLANT, rue S. Jean de Beauvais,
LAMBERT, Imprimeur - Libraire, rue & à côté
de la Comédie Françoise, au Parnasse.
}

M. D. C C L I X.

AVEC APPROBATION ET PRIVILÉGE DU ROI.

4 Women in the Enlightenment were not simply creative contributors to literature and art, but also to the exact sciences, most closely identified with 'masculine' rational reasoning. The Marquise's translation of Newton entailed much reworking of the mathematics of the original and remains the only French-language version of this pivotal text.

system based on 'Newtonian' principles of reason, order and universal law.

Newton's achievement, great though it was, also had little to say about the nature of living beings on earth itself. This was the second area towards which Enlightenment science directed much effort. How was man to understand the order of nature? Was there such an order? Were there relationships between different living beings, and, if so, of what kind? Could nature simply be understood as a two dimensional 'Great Chain of Being', stretching down from God and his angels, through to man, and in a descending order of complexity, ending in worms and stones?[12] Or were the relationships between living beings more complex?

Enlightenment natural philosophers tended increasingly to ignore those parts of the Great Chain above man, and to visualise nature, rather, as being headed by man usually represented as outside and above the natural order. Enquirers such as the Swede Linnaeus (1709–78) also started to distinguish sharply between living and non-living beings, a distinction which was to make it possible for the 'earth-sciences' such as geology and mineralogy, on the one hand, to distinguish themselves from 'life-sciences' like botany and zoology, on the other. Linnaeus and his pupils produced a new binomial classification for living beings based on their reproductive characteristics. While extremely successful in the case of plants, Linnaeus' classifications were less so in relation to other living beings. Linnaeus' approach to nature was also very largely *a*-historical, although by 1744 he was ready to speculate in his *Oratio de telluris habilitabilis incremento* (Lecture on the increase of the habitable earth) that new groups of plants and animals might have developed over time by hybridisation. But Linnaeus in the end still saw nature as a whole, as a harmonious and balanced system created by God, in much the same way that Newton's popularisers represented his view of the cosmos itself.

Linnaeus' views were challenged by the equally well-known and influential naturalist Georges-Louis Leclerc, Comte de Buffon (1708–88). In his *Histoire Naturelle*, which began publication in 1749 and rapidly became a popular publishing success, Buffon challenged the very possibility of classifying living beings in such a way as to reveal thereby the 'real' structure of nature. Whereas Linnaeus believed that species could reveal *truths* about nature, Buffon remained convinced that individuals in nature could not be classified in ways which revealed such 'truths', and that classifications were merely heuristic devices.[13]

Buffon was also much more interested than Linnaeus in the idea that

[12] The 'Great Chain' is described in A.O. Lovejoy, *The Great Chain of Being* (New York, 1936).

[13] Jacques Roger, *Buffon: un philosophe au Jardin du Roi* (Paris, 1989).

nature had a history, that its present state was not the state in which God had created it. Buffon used fossil evidence, and physical experimentation, to argue that the world and life itself were far older than was indicated by strict adherence to the chronology indicated by the account of the creation in the Book of Genesis. This importation of historical thinking into natural history has been seen by Michel Foucault as one of the essential ways in which Enlightenment science started to differ in a quite basic way from that of preceding periods, which were much more concerned to place living beings in static taxonomic relationships with each other.[14] Foucault sees this idea that nature too had a history, that species did not emerge perfect and immutable from the Divine hand, but changed in response to other pressures, over far longer periods than were indicated by current understandings of Biblical chronology, as the essential precondition for the emergence of Darwinian theory in the next century and thus for the beginning of scientific modernity. More appositely for our purposes, the question of nature's history also shows divisions emerging between the objectives of theology and scientific enquiry. Buffon's work on the rates of the earth's cooling was condemned by the Paris theology faculty, the Sorbonne, because his results implied that the earth was far older than had previously been realised, but were still reprinted in his best-selling *Epoques de la Nature* (Eras of Nature).

Still other *philosophes*, such as Diderot, applied themselves to the nature of 'life' itself, and produced a picture of 'life' as the constitutive force of nature, an impulsion within living beings themselves to survive, to reproduce, and to obey the laws of their own existence. This picture of life as a dynamic force was emphasised by Diderot, among others, and the idea of living beings as having their own purposes, or teleology, was to be advanced by Kant. Neither did much to prop up an idea of nature as fixed, immutable, perfect, and energised from outside itself, by the will of its creator in the hierarchical order of the Great Chain of Being.

By the end of the century it had become impossible to sustain the calm and stable view of nature left by many theologians. Nature began to be seen as an economy of dynamic processes, changing over time. Far from being described by a 'Great Chain' of Being, it became divided into discrete classification groups. Even man's own place in nature began to be questioned. Was man, God's highest creation, securely placed above a natural order, created for his exploitation and profit, or was he to be seen as an integral part of that order? In spite of his unique possession of a soul, after all, he also seemed startlingly similar in general conformation to the

---

[14] Foucault, *The Order of Things*. Werner's *Short Classification and Description of the Rocks* (Freiburg, 1787) suggested that geological strata followed a regular order of deposition which could be used as a guide to the history of different epochs in the history of life.

major apes. Was the earth itself still changing? If so, would it do so in a stable way? If God was benevolent and all knowing, why had so many species which he had created become extinct? The questions dragged on, with increasing resonance as the century progressed, and increasingly, especially in continental Europe, gulfs opened up between the objectives and assumptions of theology and those of 'natural philosophy'. In creating this gap, questions about the history of nature played a major role, and meant the mythical 'ordinary person's' view of nature was markedly different from what it would have been at the beginning of the century. Increasingly acceptable was the idea of nature having a history, and a long one at that, which might have seen change occurring as much by violent upheavals as by the slow accretion of the daily operations of nature. While the theological view of nature as reflecting the positive attributes of the Deity still seemed acceptable to many, especially in Great Britain, it seemed increasingly possible for men to hold simultaneously views of nature which were quite divorced from theological objectives; one where nature functioned as a secular sort of emotional therapy, and where knowledge of nature, in spite of the charges of the philosophers, had started to seem more valid and more important.

Social changes in science itself helped this process along. While it remained true well into the next century that few men could hope to make a career in full-time scientific work or even by teaching science, yet science did become much more visible and accessible. The booming publications market began to include many books of popular science, spear-headed by the popularisations of Newton discussed earlier. Popular science lectures became a regular part of urban life in Britain, the Netherlands, France and Italy.[15] In the German states, a wave of new universities founded from the 1740s onwards, like the University of Göttingen, trained future bureaucrats in forestry, agricultural science, engineering and mining, as well as in law and history. This was also the great age of the scientific society. Beginning in the 1660s, which saw the foundation both of the Royal Society of London, and the Paris *Académie des Sciences*, all over Europe, and especially in Germany and Italy, both private and publically chartered learned societies and academies sheltered and encouraged the scientific research of enthusiastic amateurs, or even, in the Paris case, of the few full-time paid workers in science.[16]

---

[15] R. Porter, 'Science, Provincial Culture and Public Opinion in Enlightenment England', *British Journal of Eighteenth-Century Studies*, 3 (1980), 16–25. Best-selling popularisations of science included the Abbé Pluche, *Spectacle de la Nature* (1732–1750).

[16] R. Hahn, *The Anatomy of a Scientific Institution: the Paris Academy of Sciences, 1666–1803* (Berkeley, 1971); R.E. Schofield, *The Lunar Society of Birmingham* (Oxford, 1963); J.E. McClellan, *Science Reorganised: Scientific Societies in the Eighteenth-Century* (New York, 1985).

Zoological gardens, and botanical gardens, such as the Jardin des Plantes in Paris directed by Buffon, allowed public access for the first time. New scientific journals were founded. Certain branches of science, particularly botany, began to be popular amongst women, who were often banned from the education in classical languages and history which was still standard for their brothers. The technological aspects of science such as forestry, mining, veterinary medicine, and agriculture began to appeal more to governments attempting to exert more control than ever over natural environments, and more than ever beset by problems in engineering, in agriculture, and in public health. By the end of the century, science had thus become implicated in the business of government itself, and especially new sciences like that of statistics and probability began to offer the possibility of controlling and predicting the need for social and natural resources on which governments depended (see Chapter 7).[17]

Paradoxically, the 'profile' of science was also raised because all this happened at a time when science was still not dominated by experimentalism. There was much rhetoric about the importance of direct observation of nature, and of careful public experimentation; but it was still perfectly possible to engage in speculative writings about Nature, such as those produced by Diderot, which were not based on an experimental approach. This was discursive science, written to be read by lay people, and diffused through the print media. The evidence of library catalogues shows that, at the beginning of the century, the most widely purchased books were theological; by the end of the century, they were fiction or popular science. Science-based crazes such as Mesmerism started to appear.[18] We may dispute Foucault's claim for the dominance of the 'taxonomic impulse' in European thought as a whole, and certainly in terms of the specific concerns of natural history. Where Foucault does appear to be on stronger ground, is with the contention that the Enlightenment earth and life sciences had a new, historical, component which was to drive a wedge between science and its former theological justifications. All this shows the extent to which science was slowly replacing religion as a dominant cultural 'plot', was inculcating as a cultural value the idea that knowledge was secular, concerned with the world as it is, and that it is to this world that men's curiosity might best be turned. Science was becoming acceptable as a form of knowledge worth

[17] L. Daston, *Classical Probability in the Enlightenment* (Princeton, 1988); G. Gigerenzer *et al.*, (eds.), *The Empire of Chance: How Probability Changed Science and Everyday Life* (Cambridge, 1989); H. Mitchel, 'Rationality and Control in French Eighteenth Century Medical Views of the Peasantry', *Comparative Studies in Society and History*, 21 (1979), 81–112.

[18] R. Darnton, *Mesmerism and the End of the Enlightenment in France* (Princeton, 1964).

pursuing in spite of both the jeers of the unlearned, and the *caveats* of the philosophers.

By the end of the century, idealisation of nature, particularly of plants and of wild mountain scenery, had come to provide a new, secular form of therapy, formerly provided by religious means for emotional disturbance. From a different direction, other forms of science – technology and statistics – began to seem increasingly important as means of control and exploitation available to governments. In spite of philosophical objections, and internal conflicts over methodology, such as the struggle between 'observation' and 'experimentation', science was increasingly successful, if not in putting forward claims to 'truth', or even, consistently to objectivity, at least in putting forward claims to both consistency, and practical utility.[19] It had begun to offer claims to control, exploit and predict nature and society, to provide secular knowledge, where man's knowledge of the universe could become independent from that of its creator. Science had come a long way from Laputa.

[19] L. Daston, 'Baconian Facts, Academic Civility, and the Pre-history of Objectivity', *Annals of Scholarship* (Spring, 1992).

5 Europe's mirror? The Enlightenment and the exotic

> What is still more to our shame as civilised Christians, we debauch their morals already too prone to vice, and we introduce among them wants and perhaps disease which they never before knew, and which serve only to disturb that happy tranquillity which they and their forefathers enjoyed. If anyone denies the truth of this assertion let him tell me what the natives of the whole extent of America have gained by the commerce they have had with Europeans.[1] (James Cook)

It is no accident that the character of Robinson Crusoe is probably the most durable literary creation of the Enlightenment. Written in 1719, the novel narrates how Crusoe finds himself cast away on a 'desert island' somewhere in the southern Caribbean. Whilst stranded there, he confronts his own true moral nature for the first time. He also gradually embarks on a programme of colonisation, beginning with agriculture, and moving his base from the beach on which he was ship-wrecked, to the centre of the island, where he feels himself 'master' of his island. After many years, his solitude on the island is broken by the arrival of a 'native', Man Friday, whom he uses as a servant: but who yet asks awkwardly penetrating questions about Crusoe's own people and beliefs.

In many respects, *Robinson Crusoe* can be seen as a parable, conscious or otherwise, of the relationship between the European Enlightenment and the rest of the world. Experience of the non-European, of different lands, climates and peoples collectively described as 'exotic', was already well established by the eighteenth century, involving economic relationships of colonisation and exploitation of both tropical nature and its human inhabitants. Colonialism, the exotic, and the exploitation of nature were inextricably linked in the eighteenth century, and provide verification of the contention that Enlightenment and the control of nature were parts of the same project. By confronting non-European lands and societies, Europeans, however, also found themselves confronting the whole question of *difference*. What was it that defined a European as *different*

---

[1] James Cook, *Journals*, ed. J.C. Beaglehole (3 vols., Cambridge, 1955–68), II, 175.

from an 'exotic'? What was it to be European? And what inconvenient questions did the different ways of exotic peoples pose to the conventions, assumptions and practices of Europeans? Was Man Friday's bewilderment when faced with ideas and practices which were normal to Crusoe, a sign perhaps that the conventions of Europe were exactly that – conventions, not rooted in 'nature', not the only right and inevitable ways of acting and believing?

Why should this theme have risen to such prominence in the eighteenth century? After all, the Enlightenment was already the heir to the prolonged European contact with exotic lands which had begun with Christopher Columbus' momentous Atlantic voyage in 1492 – and to the prolonged debates about exotic nature which had followed.[2] Eighteenth century interests in the exotic were fuelled by numerous factors which kept alive the 'exotic' as a focus of controversy even while 'the shock of the new' imported by Columbus gradually faded. First of all came the sheer interest in *difference* for its own sake, an interest which we will see displayed in the energies expended by the century in defining and enhancing differences between the genders (chapter 6). Second, came the impact of a whole new set of geographical discoveries in the eighteenth century. For the first time, through explorations by James Cook (1728–79), Louis-Anne de Bougainville (1729–1811) and others, Europeans were to gain an accurate knowledge of the one-third of the earth's surface covered by the Pacific Ocean. This 'New World of the eighteenth-century' as one historian has called it[3] was not only enormous in extent; it was also full of island peoples whose very existence had been previously unsuspected. As Bernard Smith and others have shown, images of the Pacific and its peoples became pervasive immediately afterwards both in popular prints and in high art. Cook's *Journals* of his voyages became European best sellers.[4] Quite apart too from the discoveries in the Pacific, dramatic though these were, European colonial empires in other parts of the world also expanded. The end of the Seven Years' War in 1763 had produced a transfer of colonial territory from France to Britain, which laid the basis of the expansion of colonial settlement in North America, and of colonial exploitation in the Indian sub-continent.

[2] Peter Hulme, 'The Spontaneous Hand of Nature: Sovereignty, Colonialism and the Enlightenment', in P. Hulme and L.J. Jordanova, (eds.), *The Enlightenment and its Shadows* (London, 1990); Antony Pagden, *European Encounters with the New World* (New Haven, 1993); P. Hulme, *Colonial Encounters: Europe and the Native Caribbean 1492–1797* (London and New York, 1986).

[3] Alan Frost, 'The Pacific Ocean: The Eighteenth-Century's "New World"', *Studies in Voltaire and the Eighteenth Century*, 142 (1976) 279–322; L.A. de Bougainville, *Voyage autour du Monde* (1771) ed. L. Constant (Paris, 1780); Cook, *Journals*.

[4] Bernard Smith, *European Vision and the South Pacific*, 2nd edn. (New Haven, 1988).

There was also another reason why the 'exotic' should have mattered in the eighteenth century. Definitions of Europe itself were undergoing radical change. Older ideas that Europe was able to be defined in religious terms, as 'Christendom', were being undermined.[5] As Turkish power in Europe receded from the 1690s, however, the edges of 'Christendom' became more fuzzy. If Christendom could not define itself through its difference from what many historians have described as its ultimate 'other' Islam, how was it to be defined?[6] In exactly the same way, during the Cold War, both Russia and the West, defined themselves as being that which their opponent was not. The end of that confrontation has left the identities of each far less clear. In a very similar development, after the threat from Islam receded at the beginning of the eighteenth century, Europeans became less clear about their own identity. The growing importance of Russia in the affairs of Europe also raised this question. At least nominally a Greek Orthodox state, Russia's eastern and southern borders yet trailed away into the Muslim world of central Asia, or the pagan lands of Siberia. Where did 'European' Russia end? What *was* the eastern boundary of Christendom? Could Europeans now learn more about themselves from contemplating the lives of Tahitians?

The changing religious character of Europe also changed the very nature of European concerns when faced with 'the exotic'. Post-Columbus, Europeans confronted other peoples with a complex mixture of motives and ideals, amongst which religion was strong. Especially in colonial territories owned by Catholic states like Spain, Portugal and France, missionary effort had been seen as essential to legitimate the enterprise of the conquest of exotic lands and peoples. This motive was largely absent in the eighteenth century, and this change lay at the bottom of a profound change in the issues which exotic peoples aroused for Europeans. Sixteenth- and seventeenth-century contacts with the 'exotic' had produced questions like: were Amerindians human? Did they have souls? Eighteenth-century concerns focussed on three major areas: the debate generated by idea of a 'universal' human nature; the associated debate on the meaning of human history; and the debate generated over the worth and nature of 'civilisation'.[7]

In the early part of the eighteenth century, however, the 'exotic' could still also be the well known. Though such figures as Montesquieu's Persian visitors in Paris, or Voltaire's wise Chinese mandarins, or

---

[5] Denys Hay, *Europe, the Emergence of an Idea* (Edinburgh, 1957), 118–19, points out that the Treaty of Utrecht (1713) contains the last reference to a *respublica christiana* to be found in a treaty between European states.

[6] For Islam as the 'other' see the important study by Edward Said, *Orientalism* (London, 1978).

[7] A. Pagden, *Spanish Imperialism and the Political Imagination* (New Haven, 1989).

questioning Huron Indians are used to point the strange nature of many European practices, they themselves were familiar to a western readership. Europe and Islam had joined contact well before the first millennium; an idealised vision of China had been reasonably common currency in Europe since the days of Marco Polo in the thirteenth century, or the Jesuit missions of the seventeenth. Equally familiar was their use by Enlightenment writers in ways which tended to relativise western practices, and to question their claims to being the only right or natural way to proceed.

It was really, however, more in the 1750s that questions began to emerge that involved European problems with the exotic on a deeper level. Whereas Montesquieu's Persians and Voltaire's Chinese were used in the text to question specific European practices, writers later in the century did not dwell on specific western practices, but on the whole idea of western 'civilisation'. Turning points here were Rousseau's 1750 *Discours sur les sciences et les arts* and his 1755 *Discours sur l'origine de l'inégalité parmi les hommes*.[8] Both writings, from different viewpoints, mounted an attack on 'civilisation' as inherently corrupting, involving economic development and urbanisation which multiply man's wants and 'desires' far beyond what is ethically desirable. Court society and life in crowded cities, according to Rousseau, led to moral corruption, to the moral and emotional manipulation of one man by another, so that men had to mask their 'real' feelings. Because of this, men found it difficult to express real needs, and technology, 'the arts' of Rousseau's title, existed only to multiply the objects of such inauthentic desires. In Rousseau's ideas it is easy to see the groundwork of our own debates on consumerism and technological control of nature, and it is certainly no accident that they arose in response to the increase in industrialisation and in global trade which marks the century.

Rousseau sought to answer his questions about the worth of 'civilisation' by contrasting it with a portrayal of life in 'primitive' societies. What would the life of man without the mixed benefits of western civilisation actually look like? Could existing 'exotic' peoples, living outside the urbanised civilisations of China and Persia, be taken as representing what a 'natural' man would be like? Would such a person be a 'noble savage' or would his life be as 'nasty, brutish and short', as many such as Thomas Hobbes (1588–1679) alleged that of the American Indians to be?[9] If man

---

[8] Jean-Jacques Rousseau, *Discours sur les Sciences et les Arts* (Paris, 1750); *Discours sur les origines de l'inégalité parmi les hommes* (Paris, 1755).

[9] Dryden coined the phrase in his 1670 *The Conquest of Greneda*, where a character exclaims:

> 'I am as free as Nature first made man,
> Ere the base laws of servitude began,
> When wild in woods the noble savage ran.'

is 'better' outside civilisation, then how is he to exercise his 'natural' capacities such as reason and invention without inevitably recreating the very civilisation from which he fled? In this debate, it was noteworthy that the opposite to European 'civilisation', was the 'noble savage' or 'exotic' who by definition lived closer to nature. Peoples outside Europe, apart from the Chinese, were usually seen as not having 'civilisations' of their own, but as being to greater or lesser degree in contact with 'nature'.

Much of these debates were highlighted by the Pacific discoveries of the 1770s, the first genuinely new exotics of the century. Much discussion was resumed in Denis Diderot's *Supplément au Voyage de Bougainville*,[10] written in 1772 in response to the Pacific discoveries of the French explorer Louis-Anne de Bougainville, though not published until 1796. Diderot's work moves the debate on the 'noble savage' and on 'civilisation' away from its previous implicit exotic referent of the 'savages' of the New World on to the Pacific. Diderot, like most other writers, focussed on the Tahitian islands, which rapidly became paradigmatic for Pacific peoples as a whole in European eyes. Philippe Commerson, Bougainville's naturalist, had already described Tahiti as a 'utopia', an 'elysium', where 'natural man' was born essentially good. Diderot partly continued this view of the islands as a 'utopia', and, following a Rousseauist line, saw the natives of Tahiti as better and happier, because more 'natural' than the Europeans who had discovered them.

The life of savages is so simple, and our societies are such complicated machines! The Tahitian is close to the origin of the world, while the European is closer to its old age ... They understand nothing about our manners or our laws, and they are bound to see in them nothing but shackles disguised in a hundred different ways. Those shackles could only provoke the indignation and scorn of creatures in whom the most profound feeling is a love of liberty.[11]

Diderot also saw the Tahitians as in a virtual time capsule, as being 'close to the origin of the world'. Like many Enlightenment writers, Diderot argued that 'noble savages' were like spy-glasses into the heroic phases of European culture, their simple, natural cultures replicating those of Greece and Rome in their earliest phases. In exactly the same way, the historian Jean Lafitiau had argued in his 1727 *Moeurs des sauvages américaines comparées aux moeurs des premiers temps*, that American Indian society could be seen as a living model of that of the classical world. All this meant that exotic societies, especially those viewed as having close parallels with those of Greece and Rome, were viewed by Europeans as both the ultimate 'opposite' or 'other' to themselves and yet also as a replication of Europe's own origins.

[10] Denis Diderot, *Supplément au Voyage de Bougainville* (Paris, 1796).
[11] Denis Diderot, *Le Neveu de Rameau* (1762) ed. J. Barzun and R.H. Bowen (New York, 1956), 194, 233–4.

This way of thinking about the Tahitians meant that little effort was expended in attempting to see these societies in their own terms. They were viewed very heavily through the lens of the classical past. The illustrations to James Cook's published *Journals*, for example, portrayed Pacific islanders in the poses, and with the physique, of classical statuary. When Cook's expedition first arrived on Tahiti in 1769, they gave their native hosts the names of the heroes of Greek and Roman mythology.

Such an identification between the island worlds of the Pacific and the heroic age of the classical world could also only come about because the Enlightenment viewed society and history as morality. Classical civilisation was viewed in moral terms as exemplifying a specific range of virtues, such as civic spirit, self-control, self-sacrifice and stoicism in the face of pain and danger. Once even some of these characteristics could be identified by Europeans in the exotic peoples they encountered, it was very easy to conflate their distance in space from Europe with their distance in time from the classical world. By the end of the century, the exotic was both profoundly other, and yet intimately linked to European origins.[12] This was a view especially important for those most strongly convinced of the current imperfections of European society, who found it difficult to accept the view preferred by many other Enlightenment thinkers, that history could be understood as a story of the progressive advancement of humanity.

The exotic had also become very visible in Europe. Living 'noble savages' were brought back to London and Paris. Cook returned to London from his second voyage of 1772 with a genuine Tahitian, Omai, whose simplicity, honesty, and naturalness rapidly made him the darling of London society. He was painted by the well-known artist Joshua Reynolds not in his own native dress, nor in western clothes, but in heavy draperies reminiscent of classical statuary. Bougainville did the same, bringing the Tahitian Atourou to Paris to the same enthusiastic welcome. The voyages of exploration thus not only caused a proliferation of images of the Pacific in books, plays, and pictures, but also the reassurance that 'noble savages' actually existed, and actually did display, as individuals, all the attributes distinguishing stereotypical 'primitives' from European hypocrisy and vice. In other words, Tahiti and its inhabitants came to be widely regarded as 'Utopian'. In the writings of Diderot and others, Tahiti appears as an ideal society in a beautiful landscape, a place without inequality, without sexual inhibitions or religious hypocrisy, without

---

[12] There is of course a whole history which is not explored in this chapter, which is the history of native perceptions of Europeans. An extremely thoughtful introduction to this theme is Greg Dening, *Islands and Beaches: Discourse on a Silent Land: Marquesas 1774–1880* (Honolulu, 1980).

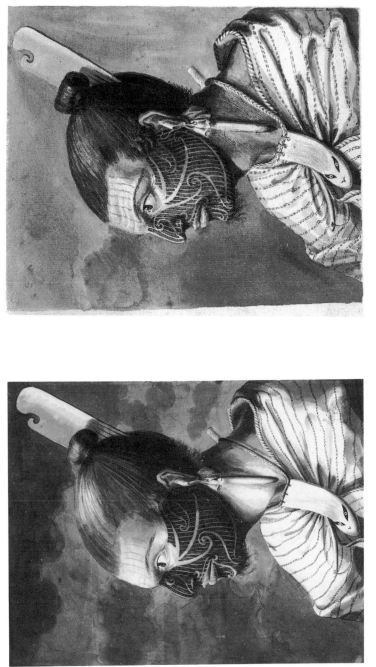

5a and 5b Two drawings of members of an exotic elite: New Zealand's Maori chiefs whose elaborate tattoos denote their high status. It was through pictures like these, by Cook's artist Sydney Parkinson, that Europeans gained their first ideas of newly discovered Pacific peoples. Here the artist emphasises the fierceness and virility of his subjects: characteristics which were often used to differentiate the warlike Maoris from other races of the region.

artificiality. Nor were these images only important for the elite. The image of Tahiti as an earthly paradise, the 'Utopia' of Phillip Commerson, was strong enough to persuade even the ordinary seamen among the *Bounty* mutineers of 1789, that Tahiti should be their chosen refuge from the world.

Why were such Utopian visions so important to the Europeans of the eighteenth century, and why were so many of them focussed on Pacific islands? Partly this happened because Christendom already possessed a long tradition of identifying Utopias with islands, from the Isles of the Blessed onwards. More specifically, for the Enlightenment, such islands appeared to prove the possibility of men actually being able to live in accordance with Enlightenment tenets. Their existence also therefore offered the promise that somehow the 'limits to Enlightenment' which we have noted elsewhere – the need to limit the potential of critique to cause unwanted social disruption – could be overcome.[13] Because the societies of the Pacific already were in full flower at the time of their discovery by Europeans, it was also possible to point to them as Utopian models, without having to pay too much attention to the issue which always dogged Enlightenment critiques, which was the problem of transition. How would it be possible for imperfect European societies to become perfected without upheaval and radical change? To point to the Pacific islands was to point to an existing Utopia unshadowed by the conditions of its production.

There was another reason for the importance of the Pacific islands in shaping European thought on the exotic. In the Pacific, geographical discoveries of new islands and continents such as Australia, by Cook, Bougainville and others was not immediately followed by colonisation and expropriation, as had been the case with the new geographical discoveries in the Americas in the sixteenth and seventeenth centuries. The Pacific islands could function there as unspoilt Utopias because discussion of them remained outside the increasing European concerns about the ethical impact of their own colonial enterprises. These were concerns which added a quite different strand to European responses to the exotic in this period.

In the early period of European colonisation in the sixteenth and seventeenth centuries, voices had indeed been raised against the cruelties to which indigenous peoples were subjected by their European masters. But few indeed had challenged the enterprise of colonisation itself, which

---

[13] Krishan Kumar, *Utopia and Anti-Utopia in Modern Times* (Oxford, 1991); G.S. Rousseau and R. Porter (eds.), *Exoticism and the Enlightenment* (Manchester, 1989); Y. Giraud, 'De l'exploration à l'Utopie: notes sur la formation du mythe de Tahiti', *French Studies*, 31 (1977), 26–41.

6 Dancing and music on the small Pacific island of Raiatea, based on a drawing by Parkinson. This depicts the aspect of the Pacific most emphasised in European images of the region as a succession of island 'utopias' discovered by Cook and Bougainville: dance, music, celebration and sensuality all mingle in this representation. Classical influences also appear especially in the piping figure on the left, modelled on the shepherds of Arcadia. The depictions of female sensuality and male strength also played into the increasing polarisation of the genders present in Enlightenment discussion.

was often legitimated by reference to the duty of Christians to spread Christ's teachings to 'the ends of the earth'. It had also been felt, and still was in the Enlightenment, that there was a positive duty for men to develop and exploit the earth's natural resources.[14] If Europeans could do this 'better' and more extensively than did native peoples, then that too justified their expropriation. In the Enlightenment, however, religious legitimations for colonisation fell out of favour. Though missionary endeavour was again to become a powerful force in colonialism in the nineteenth century, none of the great eighteenth-century voyages of exploration had religious motives. Because of this, it became much harder to justify colonialism, the enterprise which had so enlarged European notions of the exotic, by anything other than a profit motive. Also, in the absence of religious motives, enlightenment writers and practical men alike became well aware, as Cook himself had pointed out, that indigenous peoples, however idealised as 'noble savages', made only questionable gains from being 'discovered' and colonised.

Increasing questioning of colonisation itself was however marked by powerful ambivalence. Many accepted that it was a duty of man to exploit the earth's resources, or viewed commerce itself as a positive ethical value. Others realised just how much the colonial trade underpinned European prosperity in spite of increased questioning of its ethical basis, on grounds such as manifested by Cook. What would be the cost of ending colonialism? Was it practicable to do so? Others, on the opposing side, pointed out the extent to which colonial economies were only made possible by the use of slave labour. Slavery was an affront to Enlightenment ideas that there was some essential equality between human beings by virtue of, precisely, their common humanity. Its existence also challenged the increasingly important idea that human beings had universal *rights* in virtue, again, of their common humanity. Writers like Rousseau, in his *Discourse on Inequality*, pointed out that colonialism, because of the way it underpinned Western society, simply became a mechanism for the perpetuation of inequality in human society as a whole, and acted as a perpetual barrier to the realisation of Enlightenment. Racial ideas, though certainly present in this debate, played a far smaller role than they were to do in nineteenth-century approaches to the issue.[15] This was partly because slavery in the eighteenth century was far from being confined to Africans. White men were also regularly still enslaved by the Arab pirates who prowled the Mediterranean, as Defoe's Crusoe himself

---

[14] Keith Thomas, *Man and the Natural World* (London, 1976).
[15] G.W. Stocking, *Race, History and Evolution: Essays in the History of Anthropology* (New York, 1968); G. Bryson, *Man and Society: the Scottish Enquiry of the Eighteenth-century* (Princeton, 1945).

discovers. It was not so long since Cromwell had enslaved Irishmen and women, and sent them to work on the plantations of the American colonies. So it was not as easy in the eighteenth century, as it was later to become, to conflate the debate on slavery as such with a debate on race.

The *locus classicus* for Enlightenment discussions of colonialism, with all their ambivalences, is probably the massive work produced in 1770 with much assistance from Diderot by the Abbé Guillaume Thomas Raynal (1713–96), the *Histoire philosophique et politique des établissements et du commerce des européens dans les deux Indes*.[16] In spite of its prolixity, Raynal's work enjoyed instant and long-lasting success and the work penetrated far down the social scale, as Gabriel Esquer has shown. For us today it is valuable not only as a compendium of Enlightenment geographical and economic information on the colonial world, but also as a repertoire of the Enlightenment's ambivalent attitudes towards the very enterprise which underpinned its economic relationships with large areas of the non-European world. As Raynal wrote

There has never been any event which has had more impact on the human race in general and for Europeans in particular, as that of the discovery of the New World, and the passage to the Indies around the Cape of Good Hope. It was then that a commercial revolution began, a revolution in the balance of power, and in the customs, the industries and the government of every nation. It was through this event that men in the most distant lands were linked by new relationships and new needs. The produce of equatorial regions were consumed in Polar climes. The industrial products of the north were transported to the south; the textiles of the Orient became the luxuries of Westerners; and everywhere men mutually exchanged their opinions, their laws, their customs, their illnesses, and their medicines, their virtues and their vices. Everything changed, and will go on changing. But will the changes of the past and those that are to come, be useful to humanity? Will they give man one day more peace, more happiness, or more pleasure? Will his condition be better, or will it be simply one of constant change?[17]

Raynal does argue in his work for the positive moral value of colonial trade, of industry, and of the exploitation of natural resources.[18] But he is unable to argue with total conviction that 'civilised nations' have the right to colonise in the first place. He admits that in principle reason and equity do not allow us to legitimate colonisation, but then goes on to argue that in practice it can be justified in the case of previously uninhabited areas of the globe, as involving the beneficent spread of 'civilisation', or as permitting the more efficient exploitation of the land. Yet, even while

---

[16] Gabriel Esquer (ed.), *L'Anti-colonialisme au xviiè siècle: Histoire philosophique et politique des établissements et du commerce des européens dans les deux Indes, par l'Abbé Raynal* (Paris, 1951). [17] Esquer (ed.), *L'Anti-colonialisme*.
[18] E.g., *ibid.*, p. 43 (book I, ch. I, p. 1 of original text).

attempting to legitimise the colonial enterprise, Raynal still admitted that experience showed that little good had come from the contact between Europeans and native peoples. With even more confusion, Raynal argued that most native peoples were closer to nature, happier, more innocent, less corrupt, than were Europeans, were in fact morally superior; and yet that this very closeness to 'nature' which guaranteed their moral superiority, also enabled European colonisation to be justified as a way of spreading 'civilisation'. Again, Raynal manifested a very typical ambivalence on the subject of the trade in negro slaves which underpinned the labour force of the colonial plantation economies. He castigates slavery as inherently unjust, and the colonial luxury products such as sugar, tobacco and coffee as inessentials produced through the misery of slaves. He nonetheless baulked at proposals for the immediate abolition of slavery. He argued that freed slaves would not be able to use their liberty and would become a danger to themselves and to the stability of society. Where Raynal called for improvements to the lot of slaves, as he does in Book XI, he does so mainly to serve the self-interest of Europeans. Raynal's arguments, like so much of Enlightenment thought, stopped short at the point where prescription would have to turn into practice.

His ambivalence over slavery also betrayed another Enlightenment problem. Increasingly Enlightenment thinkers grounded the notion of 'rights' not in the notion of 'privilege' but in the possession of humanity itself. Persons possessed rights not because, for example, they had been born with aristocratic status and legal privileges, but because they were human. This universalist idea of rights grounded in human nature was difficult to apply. In practice, it would mean that all excluded groups, groups such as women, slaves, servants, the poor, the illiterate, could claim a share of 'rights' and hence of power, leading as the Jacobins of 1793 were to discover, to demands for equality in political participation which most were simply unwilling to contemplate in practice.[19]

As the Enlightenment increasingly grounded 'rights' in the possession of humanity, it also became increasingly important to define who and what were human. Hence it is not surprising that the Enlightenment devoted considerable attention to what we would now call issues of race, though it did so with significant differences to the way this issue was to be handled in the nineteenth and twentieth centuries. Previously, 'exotic' peoples had often been classified in terms of their customs, or religious beliefs. The Enlightenment relied to a greater extent on physical characteristics as a way of defining the boundaries and internal divisions of the human species, though without approaching Victorian levels of physical

---

[19] It is no coincidence, for example, that Mary Wollstonecraft's 1792 *Vindication of the Rights of Women* draws repeated parallels between negro slavery and female subjection.

discrimination. In this respect, the Enlightenment, as in so many others, hardly presented an agreed agenda. Some, such as the great French naturalist Georges-Louis Buffon (1707–88), argued that the human race was a unity, and that if some humans looked different from others, they did so only because of contingent factors such as climate. Buffon's work could hardly be pressed into service by anyone who wished to argue that African Negroes or American Indians were in some fundamental way different from and inferior to, Europeans. Buffon's contemporary, the Swedish naturalist Carl Linnaeus (1707–78), argued, however, in his 1740 *Systema Naturae*, that it was possible to divide man between four different classificatory groups: white Europeans, red Americans, black Africans and brown Asians. But in his 1758 edition of the same work, he introduced new groups into his classificatory analysis of the human race: wild men, pygmies and giants. Such examples show the tentative and unstable character of Enlightenment attempts to classify the members of the human race; in particular they show that physical difference was far from being the only or the most important indicator amongst humans.

Racial thinking in the Enlightenment was also complicated by arguments which were ultimately theological. Buffon's arguments for the unity of mankind would have been acceptable to those who believed that all men were ultimately descended from the original human couple, Adam and Eve, and who explained the different skin colour of African negroes by seeing it as a punishment meted out to descendants of Ham, the banished son of Noah. On the other hand, these 'monogenists' were opposed by those 'polygenists' who rejected the authority of the Biblical account, and argued that the different races of man were fundamentally different, and had sprung up independently at different times and places, some perhaps even before the creation of Adam himself. There was also a historical aspect to racial thinking. Scottish Enlightenment thinkers, such as Adam Ferguson in his 1766 *Essay on the History of Civil Society* linked differences in race with the idea that human societies all progressed through four major stages (hunting, pastoralism, agriculture and commerce).[20] Each stage, in their thinking, was characteristic of a particular race.

Controversies about the classification of man were also cut into by another debate: that concerning the superiority of the Old World over the New. John Locke's famous phrase that once, 'All the world was America' betrayed the way in which the early Enlightenment still viewed the inhabitants of the Americas (including man) as being closer to a 'state of nature' long since abandoned in Europe for the delights of 'civilisation'.

[20] Adam Ferguson, *Essay on the History of Civil Society* (Edinburgh, 1766).

Later in the century Buffon argued, on the contrary, in this 'Dispute of the New World' that American flora and fauna (including man), were smaller and inferior versions of existing European species. Far from seeing America as 'nature' to Europe's 'civilisation', Buffon and his followers emphasised an idea of American nature as a *degeneration* of its Old World counterpart. In his turn, Buffon was challenged by Rousseau, and the future US President, Thomas Jefferson, who argued that American stock was both physically more robust than European, and morally superior to it.[21]

If Enlightenment attempts to classify the varieties of mankind were inconclusive, they do at least reveal that their arguments about race were almost all very far from nineteenth-century theories which tended to a far greater degree to define racial difference in physical terms, and to see it as fundamental, intractable, and indicative of superiority and inferiority. One also has to say that Establishment debates over race were not conclusive enough either to oppose or to justify slavery. In the end, classification by natural philosophers was too inconclusive usefully to feed into debates about 'rights', or into the project of a 'science of man'. The idea of a universal human subject, could not easily be reconciled with ideas of the inferiority of the negro races, or with the justification of slavery, nor with the idea that Pacific islanders lived in a different time from westerners. Yet the very prosperity on which the rapid circulation of Enlightenment ideas depended, as we saw earlier, was sustained by a colonial trade based on the labour of slaves. It was not only Mary Wollstonecraft or Jean-Jacques Rousseau who were to see this contradiction as an essential impediment to the completion of the Enlightenment. Conflict and contradiction thus marked most Enlightenment thinking about race, as it did other aspects of the 'exotic'.

How are we to evaluate such debates? Can we say, as have Marxist historians like Michel Duchet, that the whole notion of 'primitivism', so important in the Enlightenment, of the superiority and 'naturalness' of native peoples, the whole cluster of ideas around the concept of the 'noble savage', was simply a 'cover' for the continuing exploitation of indigenous peoples in the European colonial ambit?[22] It is certainly true that even Enlightenment writers strongly committed to anti-colonial ideas, like Diderot or Raynal, stopped short of calling outright for the abolition of slavery. On the other hand, it is also true that those who in actual fact

---

[21] A. Gerbi, *The Dispute of the New World* (Pittsburgh, 1973); Thomas Jefferson, *Notes on the State of Virginia* (1785); Charles de Pauw, *Recherches philosophiques sur les Américains* (2 vols., Berlin, 1768–9); John Locke, *Two Treatises on Government* ed. P. Laslett (New York, 1965), 343; P. Honigsheim, 'The American Indian, and the Philosophy of the Enlightenment', *Osiris*, 10 (1952), 91–108.

[22] M. Duchet, *L'anthropologie et l'histoire au siècle des lumières* (Paris, 1971).

worked hardest for the abolition of negro slavery, in such pressure groups as the French *Société des Amis des Noirs* founded in 1788, or the British Society for the Abolition of the Slave Trade, founded the previous year, tended to subscribe strongly to primitivist ideas. In this sense, the Marxist case is simply not proven. What is true, is that Enlightenment ideas of the exotic as some form of Utopia especially in the case of the Pacific, may well have functioned to distract attention from the unresolved problem in Europe of just how change in the light of what Koselleck calls *critique* was to take place, and at what cost.

It may be that similar reasons explain the decline of primitivist ideas even before the French Revolution, and definitively afterwards. By the 1790s, even the image of the Pacific islanders had been tarnished by James Cook's murder on Hawaii in 1779. Concerns, long evident, about the devastating impact of European contact on native peoples, crystallised in the idea that 'primitive societies' however noble, were doomed to extinction, an idea whose repetition in our own day has been all too frequent. By 1802, Chateaubriand, the great French Romantic, could exclaim of Tahiti,

Oh, the vanity of man's pleasures! The first face one observes of their enchanted shores is that of death.[23]

If Europe looked at this point into the mirror of the exotic, the answering reflection was not comforting. Overwhelmingly, exotic peoples had not been viewed in their own terms, but in terms of Europe's concerns about itself. As Douglas Charlton puts it, for those who like Rousseau

were attacking social inequality and the evils of property or money, primitive society provided a ready instance of a better and a happier community. For those who like Diderot were attacking political tyranny, and lack of individual freedoms, it could be presented as run by mutual consent.... For those who were urging their readers to follow their own feelings, or make happiness their moral end, savages could be invoked ...[24]

Yet, by the end of the century, it no longer seemed feasible to confront the problems of European civilisation by comparing Europe with Tahiti. The 'unnatural' desires created by a corrupt urban society, and fed by industrialisation, the gap between man and nature, and the legitimation of 'rights' and personal autonomy in economic, political and emotional spheres had become problems that could no longer be exported into the metaphor of the 'exotic'. Robinson Crusoe was losing his place. Thinkers such as Johann Gottfried Herder (1744–1803) for example were beginning a systematic criticism of the way in which the Enlightenment had

---

[23] *Génie du Christianisme*, part IV, book 2, chapter 5.
[24] D. Charlton, *New Images of the Natural in France* (Cambridge, 1984), 124.

explored the crucial issues of difference in history and culture raised by the exotic in the Enlightenment. Herder challenged the optimistic view of human history as a progression towards perfection, put forward by writers such as Condorcet and Turgot. It was thought by such writers that human beings, by virtue of their humanity, could use their common possession, reason, gradually to discard irrational superstitions and customs and bring human affairs into harmony with the universal natural order. In other words, the progress of history would result in greater and greater harmonisation of human cultures, so that the world, instead of being broken by divisions between societies and cultures, would become a truly cosmopolitan whole. Many Enlightenment philosophers, such as Adam Ferguson, tended to see other, non-European cultures as merely the prior stages in development to this end. Herder strongly rejected these notions, which gave all too much support to the justification of colonialism as a way of accelerating the 'progress' of indigenous peoples by forcing European culture upon them. Herder also rejected the idea of human nature as somehow unchanged by history, geography and climate. He put forward the idea that each people develops a unique culture handed down from its forebears, as a living and evolving cultural community.

Herder thus came close to the perception that the true opposite of culture was not nature, but another and different culture. He quarrelled with

the general philosophical, philanthropic tone of our century which wishes to extend our own ideal of virtue and happiness to each distant nation, to even the remotest age of history.... it has taken words for works, Enlightenment for happiness, greater sophistication for virtue, and in this way invented the fiction of the general amelioration of the world.[25]

He believed that in this way the high-minded men of the Enlightenment had produced ideas to justify the domination of one culture over many.

The ferment of generalities which characterise our philosophy, can conceal oppressions and infringements of the freedom of men and countries, of citizens and peoples.[26]

In saying this Herder was exposing the contradiction which lay at the heart of Enlightenment thinking on other peoples, of their being viewed simultaneously as exotic and familiar, exemplary and exploitable.

Enlightenment problems in dealing with difference were not merely

[25] J.G. Herder, 'Yet Another Philosophy of History', in F. Barnard (ed.), *Herder on Social and Political Culture* (Cambridge, 1969), 187.
[26] J.G. Herder, 'Ideas for a Philosophy of the History of Mankind' in F.M. Barnard (ed.), *Herder on Social and Political Culture*, 320.

philosophical. They could result in the devastation of the non-European world. Enlightenment views of a single grand movement of progress lying behind human history could not grapple with the idea of each cultural entity being driven by its own cultural dynamic. While Herder accepted the idea of a unitary human nature he saw that human nature containing far greater potential for variability than did Condorcet. While his views are far from the later nationalistic excesses committed by his countrymen, his argument ultimately pointed out that the central failure of the Enlightenment was in the way it dealt with difference. It was this perception which was a necessary prelude to the opening of the definition of nationalism in the later nineteenth century, a task of definition which can only open as a response to previous failures to deal with the idea of 'difference' within the framework of a universal humanity.

> Who made man the exclusive judge, if woman partake with him of the gift of reason?
>
> For man and woman, truth, if I understand the meaning of the word, must be the same; yet for the fanciful female character, so prettily drawn by poets and novelists, demanding the sacrifice of truth and sincerity, virtue becomes a relative idea, having no other foundation but utility, and of that utility, men pretend arbitrarily to judge, shaping it to their own convenience.
>
> The male is male only at certain moments. The female is female her whole life ... everything constantly recalls her sex to her ... a perfect woman and a perfect man ought not to resemble each other in mind any more than in looks.[1]

The Enlightenment devoted great energies to the definition of gender, so great in fact that some historians have seen this period as a watershed in European culture's attempts to define difference between the sexes.[2] Gender, like the exotic, was an area of difference. It therefore challenged some very strong strands in Enlightenment thought, the strands that emphasised the idea of a universal human nature, and a universal human history, both validated by the possession of a single universal human form of rationality. It was no accident that by the end of the eighteenth century many thinkers such as Mary Wollstonecraft were to equate the denial of rights to slaves and the denial of rights to women. Each destabilised crucial Enlightenment assumptions. Yet in practice as well as in much

---

[1] Mary Wollstonecraft, *Vindication of the Rights of Women* [1792], ed. M.B. Kramnick (London, 1982), 87, 139; Jean-Jacques Rousseau, *Emile, ou de l'éducation* [1762] (Paris, 1964), book V, 446, 450.

[2] Rita Goldberg, *Sex and Enlightenment: Women in Richardson and Diderot* (Cambridge, 1984); Thomas Laqueur, *Making Sex: Body and Gender from the Greeks to Freud* (Cambridge, MA, 1990), 5. 'By around 1800, writers of all sorts were determined to base what they insisted were fundamental differences between the male and female sexes, and thus between man and woman, on discoverable biological distinctions, and to express these in a radically different rhetoric.'

Enlightenment writing, each was insisted upon. This chapter attempts to understand this contradiction.

A great deal of effort in the Enlightenment focussed on the definition of femininity. Images powerful in former times of women as shrews, harlots or Amazons retreated, and were replaced by numerous medical and scientific attempts to define social and cultural differences between men and women as 'natural' and therefore right and inevitable. Much debate focussed on the physical constitution of the female sex and on the importance of women's role as mothers.[3] In these debates science and medicine contributed an increasingly important voice.

Increasingly, medical writings seemed to imply that women were virtually a separate species within the human race, characterised by the reproductive functions, and by a sexuality which was often denied or repressed. Paradoxically, however, women were often ascribed the role of custodians of morality and religion within the domestic setting. This was a view of women which obviously contains many inconsistent elements. It was one which also denied women full status as individuals, at precisely the time that men were increasingly defining themselves as autonomous individual actors in the legal and economic spheres, even in those countries, such as France, whose political structures were overwhelmingly based on corporate, not individual identities.[4] Enlightenment thinking about gender thus confronted many internal inconsistencies. It set up a wide gap between the rights and autonomy increasingly demanded by men and the dependence still demanded from women. It was discrepancies such as these which were to shape the arguments which were to be put forward at the end of the century by such writers as Mary Wollstonecraft, Theodor von Hippel or the Marquis de Condorcet.[5]

Wollstonecraft's book was important, not only because of the classic status it has acquired in contemporary feminist thought, but also because it was one of the first books squarely to confront the contradictions implicit in Enlightenment ideas of gender, and point out their problems for the structure of Enlightenment thought. Wollstonecraft pointed out

---

[3] Pierre Fauchéry, *La Destinée féminine dans le roman européen du dix-huitième siècle, 1713–1807: Essai de gynécomythie romanesque* (Paris, 1972); Nancy K. Miller, The *Heroine's Text: Readings in the French and English Novel 1722–1782* (New York, 1980).

[4] Elizabeth Fox-Genovese and Eugene D. Genovese, *Fruits of Merchant Capital* (Oxford, 1983), especially chapter II 'The Ideological Bases of Domestic Economy'.

[5] Wollstonecraft, *Vindication*; Théodor von Hippel, *Uber die Bürgerliche Verbesserung der Weiber* (Berlin, 1792), reprinted Vaduz, Switzerland, 1981. Nicolas Caritat, Marquis de Condorcet, 'Lettres d'un bourgeois de New Haven', in *Oeuvres Complètes de Condorcet* (Paris, 1804), XII, 19–20; 'Déclaration des Droits: Egalité', in *Oeuvres Complètes de Condorcet*, 286–8.

that ideas of femininity supported by writers such as Rousseau, which designated women as inferior to and different from men, did nothing more, as Voltaire had previously noted, than replicate in domestic life the political system based on privilege and arbitrary power, enjoyed by monarchs and aristocrats over their subjects, or slave owners over their slaves, which those same thinkers were so ready to criticise in other contexts.[6] Wollstonecraft also identified yet more serious contradictions in Enlightenment thought as it clustered around gender. She pointed out that Enlightenment was based on ideals such as 'reason' and 'virtue' which were alleged to be innate in, or attainable by, all human beings. But rationality was precisely what was denied to women by writers such as Rousseau, and by the medical writers, while 'virtue' was defined for women in an exclusively sexual sense. As Wollstonecraft points out, however, such manoeuvres can only lead to a dangerous moral relativism which will also impede the progress of Enlightenment, by 'giving a sex to morals'.[7] By defining 'virtue' as one thing for men and another for women, any attempt to link Enlightenment and religion could also be undermined. As she points out, even:

If women are by nature inferior to men, their virtues must be the same in quality, if not in degree, or virtue is a relative idea . . . virtue has only one eternal standard[8]

it is a farce to call any being virtuous whose virtues do not result from the exercise of its own reason.[9]

To say that virtue for some human beings (women) is not founded on rationality and is differently defined from that practised by other human beings (men) is to give it characteristics which mean it cannot grow from God, since he is one, eternal and rational.

If women were in fact not rational, Wollstonecraft argued, it would be far preferable to abandon pretence, and exclude them altogether from social life, in the same way that animals are. If they *are* rational, then they should take part in the same moral and intellectual life that men do:

Contending for the rights of woman, my main argument is but on this simple principle, that if she be not prepared by education to become the companion of man, she will stop the progress of knowledge and virtue: for truth must be common to all, or it will be inefficacious with respect to its influence on general practice.[10]

Without a universal, non-gendered standard of morals and rationality, it would not be possible to sustain the Enlightenment project of emancipation through universal value systems based on reason and virtue, if one-

---

[6] Wollstonecraft, *Vindication*, 121–2.   [7] *Ibid.*, 121.   [8] *Ibid.*, 108; see also 109, 139.
[9] *Ibid.*, 103.   [10] *Ibid.*, 86.

half the human race were held to lack a capacity for either quality. In other words, the way the Enlightenment thought about gender contradicted, undermined, and challenged its claims to legitimacy as a universally applicable project.

It has often been pointed out that many of these contradictions arose from the way in which the Enlightenment connected discussion of gender with the ambiguous concept of nature. The concern of Rousseau and others like him was to define femininity as 'natural' and hence as both 'right' and ineluctable. In doing so, they were attaching the debate on femininity to one of the central concerns of the Enlightenment. 'Natural' could mean many different things: it could mean 'not socially defined'; not 'artificial'; 'based on the external physical world'. Overwhelmingly, 'natural' was used, often in a mixture of all these meanings, to legitimate and control arrangements which we in the twentieth century would see as socially created, and hence subject to change and criticism.[11] 'Naturalness' was also often used to legitimate arguments aimed to bring into being a state of affairs which did not yet fully exist. 'Natural' in other words was a very good way to argue for points of view that were in fact often novel and always highly prescriptive. Social arrangements could be given additional validation by being presented as 'natural'. Arguments for the 'naturalness' of feminine roles could thus, because of the ambiguity of the term, gain force from biological arguments about created 'nature', and, at the same time, from repeated Enlightenment polemics against 'artificiality' in society, by which was meant social practices which were held to be at odds with the 'real' or true structures of 'human nature'.[12]

The extreme ambiguity of the term 'nature', could be thus used in multiple ways to define femininity in this period. Women were increasingly defined as closer to 'nature' than were men, as well as being more determined by 'nature', meaning anatomy and physiology. Women were especially affected by a definition of 'nature' as meaning the external, created world, as that realm upon which mankind acts, partly to manipulate, partly to render intelligible. 'Nature' could be taken to be that part of the world, which human beings have understood, mastered and made their own.[13] Equally the notion that women are closer to nature than men included *both* the claim that because of their physical 'nature' they were emotional, credulous, and incapable of objective reasoning; and at the

[11] L.J. Jordanova, *Sexual Visions: Images of Gender in Science and Medicine between the Eighteenth and Twentieth Centuries* (London and New York, 1989), 19–42, esp. 41.
[12] The most celebrated controversy of the Enlightenment on this issue was that caused by Rousseau's own 1750 *Discours sur les sciences et les arts*.
[13] Jordanova, *Sexual Visions*, 41.

same time that they were the carriers, within the family, of a new morality through which the *un*-naturalness of civilisation, its artificiality, could be transcended and a society created which was natural, polite and modern.[14] Cultural images of this complex relation between femininity and the natural could range from the ultimate subjection of superstition by reason, and women by men in Mozart's opera *The Magic Flute* (1791), or in the promises of regeneration *through* women expressed in Bernadin de St-Pierre's 1788 best-seller *Paul et Virginie*:

Women lay down the first foundations of natural laws. The first founder of a human society was a mother of a family. They are scattered among men to remind them that above all they are men, and to uphold, despite political laws, the fundamental law of nature . . . Not only do women bind men together by the bonds of nature, but also by those of society.[15]

However, in spite of all these ambiguities, one point clearly stands out. In spite of the Enlightenment tendency to define the 'natural' as 'the good', women's equation with 'nature' did not operate in such a way as to give her equality with or superiority over men: rather, paradoxically, it operated to place women at one remove from men, to define them as 'the other': as that which has to be defined, rather than that whose nature is obvious and right. It is also important that once the definition of 'femininity' and of 'nature' are brought together, each becomes problematic. Why should women be more 'natural' than men? Especially at a time when, in other contexts, humanity as a whole was often urged in the Enlightenment to abjure artificiality and convention, and become more 'natural'. The important point here is that the project of defining femininity perturbs and renders problematic very many key Enlightenment concepts, like 'nature'.

Perhaps it was an attempt to tie down 'nature' that led to such interest in the Enlightenment in scientific and medical definitions of gender. Recently, historians such as Thomas Laqueur have argued that between the seventeenth and eighteenth centuries, the definition of male and female began to undergo a redefinition much influenced by medical definitions of the gendered body. A rising cultural status for science and medicine, allowed the 'truths of biology' to replace

divinely ordained hierarchies or immemorial custom as the basis for the creation or distribution of power in relations between men and women.[16]

[14] Sylvana Tomaselli, 'The Enlightenment Debate on Women', *History Workshop Journal*, 20 (1985), 101–24. Women's role in creating a new and decent society was especially emphasised in the context of the American Revolution: Jan Lewis, 'The Republican Wife: Virtue and Seduction in the Early Republic', *William & Mary Quarterly*, 44 (1987), 689–721.

[15] J.H. Bernadin de St. Pierre, *Paul et Virginie* (Paris, 1788); preface to 1806 edition.

[16] Laqueur, *Making Sex*, 193.

Put briefly, older ideas that the female body was essentially another version of that of the male, with the female organs of reproduction being seen as inversions or homologies of male equivalents was replaced, Laqueur argues, by the idea that male or female bodies were absolutely different.[17] In anatomy, structures that had been thought common to men and women, like the skeleton and the nervous system, were now differentiated. Organs such as ovaries and testes, which had previously shared a name, were now separately labelled.[18] Anatomical studies on women's brains argued that they were of smaller size, and thus conclusively demonstrated women's unfitness for intellectual pursuits.[19] Many women themselves seem to have accepted these ideas. For example, in direct response to Wollstonecraft's *Vindication*, Laetitia Hawkins stated in her 1793 *Letters on the Female Mind*:

It cannot, I think, be truly asserted, that the intellectual powers know no difference of sex. Nature certainly intended a distinction ... In general, and almost universally, the feminine intellect has less strength and more acuteness. Consequently in our exercise of it, we show less perseverance and more vivacity ...[20]

Writers like Hawkins were by the 1790s only echoing very similar ideas used by influential writers like Jean-Jacques Rousseau earlier in the century. Describing Sophie as the 'ideal woman' he created in his educational tract *Emile* (1762), Rousseau talks of the way in which Sophie's physical make-up both sharply distinguishes her from Emile, her intended mate, and operates to ensure firstly her subjection to him, and secondly her definition as maternal and domestic:

The male is male only at certain moments; the female is female her whole life ... everything constantly recalls her sex to her, and to fulfill its functions, an appropriate physical constitution is necessary to her ... she needs a soft sedentary life to suckle her babies. How much care and tenderness does she need to hold her family together! ... The rigid strictness of the duties owed by the sexes is not and cannot be the same.[21]

For writers like Rousseau, basing themselves on the implications of contemporary medical texts, women's occupations 'were taken to be

---

[17] Laqueur, *Making Sex*, 149–50.
[18] Londa Schiebinger, 'Skeletons in the Closet: The First Illustrations of the Female Skeleton in Eighteenth-Century Anatomy', *Representations* 14 (1986), 42–82; *The Mind Has No Sex? Women in the Origins of Modern Science* (Cambridge, MA., 1989), 191–200; Laqueur, *Making Sex*, 152. The second half of the article 'Squelette' in Diderot's *Encyclopédie* is entirely devoted to the female skeleton.
[19] Elizabeth Fee, 'Nineteenth-Century Craniology: The Study of the Female Skull', *Bulletin of the History of Medicine*, 53 (1979), 415–33; Schiebinger, 'Skeletons', 206–7.
[20] Letitia Hawkins, *Letters on the Female Mind* (London, 1792).
[21] Rousseau, *Emile*, 450.

rooted in, restricted to, and a necessary consequence of their reproductive functions'.[22]

The fact that ideas of gender *could* be discussed in this way is also an important pointer to the way in which thinking about gender in the twentieth century differs from that of the eighteenth. In our own day, most people have come to believe that differences between the genders are due as much, if not more, to differences in training, education and social expectations than they are rooted in the different biology of men and women. For the Enlightenment, on the other hand, biological difference and culturally induced sex roles were seen as one and the same thing. For most eighteenth-century thinkers, biological difference *directly* generated the social roles assigned to each sex, such as the increasing stress on women's unique fitness for the role of wife and mother. Another crucial difference with our own way of thinking, is the explicit generalisation of gender roles, whereas today it is often stated that each individual is unique in his or her mixture of 'masculine' or 'feminine' attributes.

Laqueur's arguments, and those of the historians who follow his lead, about the increasing tendency to define gender as absolute difference through biological and medical 'evidence' sound convincing. But do they cover the entire problem of changes in thinking about gender in this period? We may point out, first of all, that Laqueur admits quite freely that we shall probably never know how many people actually believed the scientific and medical theories put forward to redefine femininity.[23] He himself points out that many older beliefs about gender seem to have co-existed with the Enlightenment redefinitions.[24] The increasing differentiation between physiological models of male and female produced by medical and scientific literature co-existed, for most people outside the elites addressed by medical arguments, with much older ideas of masculinity and femininity. As Laqueur also admits, the new, medically driven ideas of sexual difference, also did not derive from a scientific consensus based on overwhelming evidence. No single account of sexual difference triumphed and new knowledge about human anatomy and physiology did not support the claims about gender difference which were made.[25] It is not logically possible to move from the 'Is' of scientific fact to the 'Ought' of gender roles in society: or put in another way, from the descriptive to the prescriptive. Laqueur does not really tackle the question of why it was, in that case, that eighteenth-century writers expended so much

---

[22] L. Jordanova, *Sexual Visions: Images of Gender in Science and Medicine between the Eighteenth and Twentieth Centuries* (London and New York, 1989), 29: 'Women's capacity to bear and suckle children was taken to define their physical, psychological and social lives'. See also Yvonne Knibichler, 'Les médecins et la 'nature féminine' au temps du Code Civil', *Annales*, ESC, 31(1976), 824–45.

[23] Laqueur, *Making Sex*, 152.   [24] Laqueur, *Making Sex*, 153–54.

[25] Laqueur, *Making Sex*, 152.

energy in making precisely this connection between the different biological nature of women and their social roles. Many historians have pointed to large-scale industrial change and development as the motor for changes in women's social roles. They argue that industrialisation and the construction of global markets necessitated the construction of a 'sexual division of labour' which assigned to women, especially middle-class women, the task of consuming the increased array of goods made available by industrialisation.[26] This 'division of labour', they argue, led inexorably to the construction of a 'domestic sphere' which was to be the main place of consumption, and peculiarly the domain of women. Such historians also point out, as Laqueur does not, that much Enlightenment thinking about women's biological nature was inherently class based; that what was being described in the medical accounts of the female body, was not the body of *all* women, and certainly not the bodies of hardworking farm women or urban artisans, but much more the frail and soft bodies which could with more plausibility be ascribed to middle-class women. Some historians like Nancy Armstrong, have carried this argument so far as to assert that the new economic role assigned to domestic, middle-class women meant that the first truly modern economic person was a female, because the female role was the first to be described as an economic function.[27]

However, the idea that women's sphere was the domestic world was hardly new in the eighteenth century, and had frequently been stated in historical eras which long antedated either industrialisation or the biological redefinition of femininity.[28] What had changed in the Enlightenment was the increasing reliance on medical 'evidence' to back up this idea. It must always be noted that such medical justifications also co-existed with much older justifications for women's role as defined by their family responsibilities, through the means of scriptural injunctions, and traditional precedent. Historians who thus emphasise the Enlightenment attitude to gender as unique or new, thus often encounter real problems in justifying their views in the light of specific historical contexts in the eighteenth century. It is also far from clear that the majority of women even in the middle and upper classes which were most exposed to such

---

[26] E.g., Fox-Genovese and Eugene Fox-Genovese, *Fruits*; V. Jones, *Women in the Eighteenth Century: Constructions of Femininity* (London, 1990); J.B. Elshtain, *Public Man, Private Woman* (Oxford, 1981).

[27] N. Armstrong, *Desire and Domestic Fiction: A Political History of the Novel* (Oxford, 1987).

[28] Steven Ozment, *When Fathers Ruled: Family Life in Reformation Europe* (Cambridge, Mass., 1983); B. Niestroj, 'Modern Individuality and the Social Isolation of Mother and Child', *Comparative Civilisation's Review*, 16 (1987), 23–40 points out the medieval and early Renaissance roots of much that has been taken to be specific to Enlightenment ideologies of gender, and materialism.

debates on 'women's role' in society, and on the definition of femininity, really accepted such teachings and allowed them to influence their lives. Great controversy surrounded even the 'new' social role for women as wife and mother which many historians have seen as central to the redefinition of femininity in this period.[29]

Women's economic role was increasingly replaced by an emotional one, and the image of woman 'naturally' fitted for domestic duties particularly of providing warm maternal care to her children, and loving companionship for her spouse, was increasingly argued for by eighteenth-century writers, and depicted by artists.[30] Such theorists of the family paid particular attention to the practice of wet-nursing or sending infants, often to distant villages, to be suckled and cared for by paid foster-mothers. This practice was current in continental Europe, and involved all social classes except the very poorest. Historically already well-established by the Enlightenment, it was to survive as a socially acceptable practice in France, at least, right up to 1914.[31] In the 1760s, however, writers such as Rousseau increasingly argued against it. In his *Emile*, Rousseau echoed many contemporaries when he argued that mothers who sent their children away to be nursed were 'unnatural', rejecting the duties of maternity which her physiological construction indicated to her:

The sweet mothers who give themselves over to the gay pleasures of the town, do they pause to think what treatment their children are receiving in their swaddling bands out in the villages?[32]

Yet this was an ideology, which those women who absorbed these diatribes in favour of maternal breast feeding obeyed at some cost. As Rousseau made clear, the price of a clear maternal conscience on the matter of breast feeding and intimate maternal relationships with infants and small children, was increased confinement within the family circle, in exchange for freedom to taste the attractions of the city, the world outside the family.

Rousseau's arguments, and the arguments of the many writers whom

---

[29] D.G. Charlton, 'The New Eve', in *New Images of the Natural in France: A Study in European Cultural History 1750–1800* (Cambridge, 1984); Mary Sheriff, 'Fragonard's Erotic Mothers and the Politics of Reproduction', in L. Hunt (ed.), *Eroticism and the Body Politic* (Baltimore and London, 1991), 14–40; Carole Duncan, 'Happy Mothers and Other New Ideas in French Art', *Art Bulletin*, 55 (1973), 570–83.

[30] Sherriff, 'Fragonard's Erotic Mothers'; Duncan, 'Happy Mothers'.

[31] Mary Lindeman, 'Love for Hire: The Regulation of the Wet-Nursing Business in Eighteenth-Century Hamburg', *Journal of Family History*, 6 (1981), 379–95; G. Sussman, *Selling Mother's Milk: The Wet-Nursing Business in France, 1715–1914* (Urbana, IL., 1982).

[32] Rousseau, *Emile*, 45.

he echoed are also interesting in another way. The versions of femininity they argue for can often be shown to have far older roots. But it is certainly also the case that arguments about gender do intersect with other concerns in Enlightenment thinking in ways which *are* specific to that period. This is an important point to make, because it allows us to pinpoint better ways of saying that the Enlightenment *did* bring something new to debates on gender, and secondly to say why it was that such debates were of consequence in the overall pattern of Enlightenment thinking.

It was not simply that the problem of gender disturbed some of the deep structures of Enlightenment thought. That was also true of the way in which any group conceived of as 'different', such as non-European peoples, or the poor, could also only be received with difficulty into Enlightenment universalism. It was also the case with women, however, that it was far less easy to *exclude* the problem of gender because women themselves persisted in participating in the formation of Enlightenment culture. The eighteenth century saw the emergence, for the first time, of a sizeable body of women earning an independent living by various forms of cultural production, whether as members of 'Grub Street', as free intellectuals such as Mary Wollstonecraft herself, or as painters such as Angelica Kauffman or Elizabeth Vigée-Lebrun. Such independent women, as was remarked in chapter 2, posed a major problem for the emerging independent male intellectual class. As women, they were defined as intellectually inferior and intrinsically lacking in the social and political authority which they implicitly laid claim to by the very act of writing. The numerous aggressive attacks on women's intellectual capacities and specifically on women's writing produced by male intellectuals, show their worry that women's admission to the ranks of independent intellectuals might tar their male colleagues with the stigma of dependency and irrationalism which was so commonly alleged to be an intrinsic part of the female character by writers such as Rousseau. So 'gender' was not simply a difficult topic for reflection by the Enlightenment, it was also a theme which affected who and what the Enlightenment thought it was. Was it genuinely a movement of autonomous, rational, objective, hence legitimate, and hence also male thinkers, whose right to criticise the order of society lay in the very characteristics which also defined their male gender; or did it also include women, the reverse of the masculine? For the thinkers of the Enlightenment, the question raised by Mary Wollstonecraft of whether rationality *was* a universal human characteristic or was confined only to men, was a profoundly political as well as a philosophical one: because in the answer to that question lay the entire right of the *philosophes* to carry out the business of *critique* with legitimacy.

7 The Marquise du Châtelet, author of an important translation of
Newton's *Principia Mathematica*, and companion of Voltaire. Well
illustrates the increasing, if often questioned, contribution of women
to the formation of ideas, and the web of personal relationship uniting
Enlightenment thinkers.

Women in the Enlightenment did, however, carry out more traditional roles which connected them both to the production of 'opinion' and 'knowledge', as well as to the 'public realm' theorised by Habermas (chapter 1). Women were crucial to the organisation of one of the most characteristic intellectual institutions of the Enlightenment in continental Europe: the *salon*. Our analysis so far of the economic structures and the sociability crucial to the making and diffusion of Enlightenment ideas has emphasised so far public, commercial, and predominantly male-controlled markets for ideas, and diffusion networks. The *salons* were quite other. The *salon* as a social form concerned with ideas had its roots in the seventeenth century, and in court society, particularly in France. Aristocratic ladies had begun to gather around themselves groups of both women and men, often of a somewhat lower status than themselves, and to encourage the production within and by those groups of an elaborate, literary, common culture. Members of the groups met to discuss topics often designated in advance by the *salon* hostess. Plays, poems and prose works were produced, read aloud in the groups, and often substantially altered in response to criticism by other *salon* members before being presented to a wider public. For some, *salon* presentation was seen not merely as an essential part of the creative process, but as an acceptable equivalent to publication in print. *Salons* in the seventeenth century were thus crucial because they set intellectual agendas, and provided a social forum for what often amounted to group literary and intellectual production, amongst the social elite. In all this, women were crucial. Each *salon* was a distinctive creation of the hostess, with its own character and programme, and group culture. It was the hostess who provided the meeting place for the group, usually in the family residence. It was she (or indirectly her husband) who met the costs of entertainment. It was she who chose the members of the *salon*, and oversaw the relationships they formed; it was she who largely controlled thereby the intellectual agendas of the group. The social status of the salon hostess, in other words, as well as her financial capital, legitimated the intellectual production of the *salon* members, who tended to be of a lower social class. The *salons* also thereby legitimated the intellectual style, and agendas of their women members. In the seventeenth century, such female *salon* hostesses and female members were often described as *précieuses*, women whose particular, distinctive, highly mannered and controlled way of speaking and writing, whose prediction for verbal gaming, was the high point of development of the distinctive literary culture of the *salon*.

By the eighteenth century, therefore, the *salon* already had a long history, and a history which enshrined women as shapers of elite culture. The *salon* by this point had also begun to create a common verbal, literary, allusive culture which helped to eliminate the gulf between the sexes caused by their very different educations and social roles. But the eighteenth century saw also significant changes for the *salons*. They began to move out of court society. The aristocratic hostess began to be replaced by women like Mme du Deffand, wife of a successful financier, or Mme du Tencin, D'Alembert's mother, whose reputation as a novelist was only exceeded by the scandal which surrounded her, and effectively excluded her from the court; or Julie de Lespinasse, the beloved of D'Alembert, and poor relation and protégée of Mme du Deffand. Many of the functions of the hostess in recruiting and organising the *salons*, setting their agendas, and managing the personal relationships of their members, remained the same. But their wider social basis during the Enlightenment, manifested how, very gradually, control of intellectual agendas, was passing from the court to a far wider social and intellectual elite. It also meant that the *salons* were able to bring into their membership many who like Diderot began life outside the aristocratic, legal, or administrative *elites*. By *salon* membership such non-elite members, not only gained audience for, and contribution to their own work, but also access to a social capital of relationships which could allow them ascension into the elite itself through the operation of patronage. It was also the case that the increasing numbers of non-aristocratic *salons* widened the intellectual agenda from the culture of the *précieuses*, to a wider focus on critical writing in history, economics and politics, from the word game to the message itself. In this way, the changing focus of the *salon* mirrored the changing orientation of cultural creation as a whole, whose project was decreasingly aimed at the capture of the apex of the social and political pyramid and increasingly at the more and more heterogenous elites who shaped public opinion outside the reach of the court. The court had ceased to be the single most significant arbiter of and actor in the public realm. This erosion of the intellectual dominance of the court happened at the same time as the erosion of its political control. This was no coincidence.

But what was the importance of gender in the *salons*? Why did they remain a powerful force at a time when so much else in the way that culture was transmitted and created seemed to be defined in such a different way, and defined in ways which undermined women's cultural and intellectual roles? Partly, the *salons* remained as a viable social and intellectual form because of the very expansion of the surrounding public realm. Increasing number of career intellectuals born well outside the old court aristocracy needed a mechanism for the social ascension which would allow them to transform their gifts into visible social and political recognition. Nor was the 'collective' creation characteristic of salon culture incompatible with eventual publication for a broad market; it could even be seen as a safe way of advance testing audience reaction. But why do women, and not men, emerge as the *salon* organisers? A large part of the answer to this should refer back to the discussion of gender earlier in the chapter. This was partly because of the way women's role had been defined in the eighteenth century in ways which in fact were far wider than their reproductive roles: as being the agents and bearers of the civilised state, whether through their role as actual mothers or as intellectual mothers transmitting cultural values to the next generation. This role as the organiser, facilitator, and if necessary inspirer of male knowledge production is of course as old as that of the nine muses. But it was also a role which women, whose intellectual independence was challenged in other ways, as we have already seen, could turn into one which put them into close contact with other intellectual figures, contact necessary for the enhancement of their own public careers and yet leave them in control of the (predominantly male) members of the *salon*. The increasing numbers of women who, as the seventeenth-century hostesses had in the main not been, were literary producers as well, shows that women were realising the flexibility of the role of the *salonnière* to place a purchase on the intellectual community which might well otherwise have been denied them on grounds of their sex.

It may be because of the nature and antecedents of the *salon*, with its legacy of feminine dominance and of the *précieuses'* interest in elaborate, artificial, language, that the *salons* also attracted the wrath of political writers such as Rousseau. Rousseau inveighed against the *salons* because of these very factors, their feminine dominance, historical links with a decaying and highly artificial court culture, were enough to attract his anger. For him, their artificiality was an open affront to the transparency and 'naturalness' which ought to govern human relations as well as define the human polity. For the same reasons, Rousseau also inveighed against the public theatre. For those who like Rousseau believed that women were dominated by their sexual and reproductive roles, women controlling any social institution was equivalent to it being riddled with sexual corruption. His attacks on the *salons* thus also fed into the increasing propensity to define the monarchy itself as corrupt because of the alleged dominance of its policy by women's sexual bargaining. The polemic over women's intellectual role and capacities in the Enlightenment was therefore intimately linked with attempts to reshape the very culture and power relationships of government itself, which as we will see in the next chapter was a strong concern in the Enlightenment.

Recent historical scholarship, while usefully highlighting the importance of biological definitions of female 'nature' as well as indicating new, if controversial, ways in which economic change may have contributed to the Enlightenment redefinition of gender has also perhaps neglected the complexity of the Enlightenment response to this issue. The stress which the gender debate placed on key concepts such as 'nature', was mirrored by intense discussion on femininity which was neither so concerned with biology or economics, nor so avowedly restrictive as current emphases on Rousseau's teachings in *Emile* would have us believe. We should not forget, after all, that *Emile* was condemned upon publication by the Paris Parliament, and publicly burnt (although not because of its view on gender), and remained controversial, ever after. In fact, the views of other *philosophes* on women, were very different.[33] Voltaire, Montesquieu and Diderot all noted the discrepancy between the legal codes which excluded women from any position in public life, and the actual extent of the power women were capable of wielding.[34] Diderot, unlike the doctors and natural scientists, argued that men and women were not very different, though certain characteristics were more often found in one sex than the other.[35] In the realm of intellect, Voltaire maintained, unlike Rousseau, that 'women are capable of all that men are'. Such views did not stop such men of letters justifying a double standard of sexual morality, justified by women's special role in the family, but they did show a most un-Rousseau-like concern with moving towards an affirmation of the common humanity of men and women, which should over-ride the reproductive roles so stressed by Rousseau and the medical definitions of femininity. Voltaire objected to the idea of the husband as sole master in the home; he, Diderot and Montesquieu, pictured maternity not as a woman's whole character but as a single and temporary aspect of life.[36] Recognition of such thinking can act as a valuable corrective to concerns now current in historical and literary scholarship relating to gender in the Enlightenment.

Conclusion

The Enlightenment debate on gender was conducted with such energy because of the contradictions and challenges it imported into the heart of Enlightenment thinking. Examination of the debates around gender shows us that Enlightenment, for all its universalist claims, had much

---

[33] Paul Hoffman, *La Femme dans la pensée des Lumières* (Paris, 1977); Hunt, M. *et al.* (eds.), *Women and the Enlightenment* (New York, 1984), survey the often contradictory attitudes of the Enlightenment towards women.

[34] F.M.A. de Voltaire 'Femmes, soyez soumises à vos maris', *Dialogues et anecdotes philosophiques*, ed. Raymond Nares (Paris, 1955), 216; Denis Diderot, 'Sur les femmes', *Oeuvres*, ed. André Billy (Paris, 1951), 985.

[35] Diderot, 'Sur les femmes'.

[36] Diderot, 'Sur les femmes'; Voltaire, 'Femmes, soyez soumises'; Montesquieu, *Spirit of the Laws*, Book XXIII, I (Paris, 1748).

difficulty in finding a place for social groups – not just women, but also lower social classes, and other races – which previous historical periods had equally defined as outside the central human community. In the case of women, the problem of the definition of gender cut across such key Enlightenment terms as 'nature', 'reason' and 'virtue'. With particular insistence new attempts were made to present social differences between the genders as based on 'natural', physiological and medical 'facts'. This showed a new tendency for social debates to be legitimated by science in a way which was to become commonplace in the following century. By problematising women's intellectual capacities, Enlightenment debates also introduced fractures into the 'republic of letters' or 'public opinion'. All these fractures, as Wollstonecraft noted, made it difficult to sustain Enlightenment claims to be the 'party of humanity', sustained by the universal project of reason and virtue.

Furthermore, such claims also rendered the place of women in public life highly problematic. Enlightenment thinkers seemed to assert, on the one hand, that women, as human beings, could have rights; but also, on the other, that because of their alleged irrationality and lack of autonomy, they should not be allowed to take part in politics.[37] Writers such as Rousseau went further, and argued that women's participation in politics was actively harmful. Such assertions fed into a rising tide of hostility especially in France, directed at the real if informal power, enjoyed by women royal favourites, and towards Queens such as Marie Antoinette.[38]

As a resource for the future, the Enlightenment showed similar ambiguities. The practice of the Enlightenment set the stage for the creation of an entirely masculine political culture during the French Revolution; but its theory of universalism also gave ammunition to those who were to struggle to free women from restrictive definitions of gender.[39] The debate over women thus contributed to the reshaping of power in the Enlightenment which is the subject of the next chapter.

[37] This argument is developed most recently in Joan Landes, *Women and the Public Sphere in the Age of the French Revolution* (Ithaca and London, 1988). Writers like Diderot who commended the work of exceptional female rulers such as Catherine the Great of Russia, still argued that women should be subject to husbands.

[38] Sara Maza, 'The Diamond Necklace Affair Revisited (1785–86): The Case of the Missing Queen', in L. Hunt (ed.), *Eroticism and the Body Politic* (Baltimore, 1991), 63–89; Sara Maza, 'Le Tribunal de la Nation', *Annales ESC*, 42(1987), 73–90.

[39] D. Outram, *The Body and the French Revolution: Sex, Class and Political Culture* (New Haven and London, 1989).

7   Enlightenment and government: new departure or business as usual?

A properly constituted state must be exactly analogous to a machine, in which all the wheels and gears are precisely adjusted to one another, and the ruler must be the foreman, the mainspring, or the soul – if one may use the expression – who sets everything in motion. (Johann von Justi)

Absolute monarchies are but one step away from despotism. Despotism and Enlightenment: let anyone who can try to reconcile these two. I can't.   (Franz Kratter (1787))

I go about, I learn, I see, I inform myself, and I make notes. That's more like being a student than a conqueror   (Joseph II (1773))[1]

A major theme of this enquiry so far has been the relationship between knowledge, critical reflection and power. As we have seen, it was not only philosophers like Immanuel Kant who reflected on the lengths to which unlimited Enlightenment could be taken, before it began to disrupt, rather than illuminate, the structures of society. In this chapter we confront the issue in the most direct way. We examine the extent to which Enlightenment ideas were used by governments in this period, and what impact if any these ideas had not only on government policy, but also on the nature of government itself. We will see if debates on government intervention in the economy, and in church–state relations as well as much wider ranging controversy on what constituted legitimate government, may have prepared the way for the wave of revolutionary movements which accompanied the Enlightenment and which was to culminate in the upheavals in France from 1789 onwards. We will also try to establish how Enlightenment ideas helped or hindered rulers in their search for international success, and internal stability and prosperity.

These are complex questions, not least because the constant flux affecting the exercise of power is not peculiar to the eighteenth century.

---

[1] Johann von Justi, quoted in G. Parry, 'Enlightened Government and Its Critics in Eighteenth Century Germany', *Historical Journal*, 6 (1963), 182; Franz Kratter, *Philosophische und statistische Beobachtungen vorzüglich die Österreichischen Staaten betreffend* (Frankfurt and Leipzig, 1787), 23–4; Joseph II quoted in D.E.D. Beales, *Joseph II* (Cambridge, 1987) I, 361.

Rulers have always striven to make their lands stable, secure, and prosperous. We may find it hard therefore to distinguish how the Enlightenment made a specific contribution. Historians in fact have expended much ink for over a century in trying to come to grips with the problem, although it is difficult to say that this historiographical legacy has in fact been successful in enhancing our understanding.

In the nineteenth century, German historians such as Wilhelm Roscher and Reinhold Koser began to use the label 'Enlightened Absolutism' to refer to a form of monarchy, heavily influenced by Enlightenment ideas, whose emergence they discerned particularly in the German states, and especially in the Prussia of Frederick II. Roscher argued that Enlightened Absolutism represented the final stage in the evolution of monarchy since the confessional conflicts of the sixteenth century. Efforts by monarchs in that period to anchor their authority in imposing confessional unity on their subjects, had, Roscher argued, been replaced in their turn by monarchs such as Louis XIV who represented themselves as sole and absolute public representatives of their peoples. By the eighteenth century, Enlightened Absolutism would lead to the emergence of the idea of the ruler being the 'first servant of his people' in the words of Frederick II.[2]

This conceptualisation of the relationship between Enlightenment and monarchy, however, attracted very little attention in western Europe. After the First World War, new attempts were made to define this relationship. The International Commission on Historical Sciences, searching for a unifying theme for its membership, established an international research project on what it chose to label 'Enlightened Despotism'. Its 1937 report on this theme, and particularly the overview produced by the ICHS Secretary, Michel L'Héritier, produced a concept of the relationship between Enlightenment and government, largely conceived as the impact of French thinkers on monarchies, which was widely influential.[3]

After 1945, the concept of 'Enlightened Despotism' came increasingly under attack. Anachronism was one charge: no eighteenth-century ruler used the term to describe themselves. Ambiguously formulated by the French writer Mercier de la Rivière in his 1767 *L'ordre naturel et essential des sociétés politiques* its use was very uncommon in the eighteenth century.[4] Whatever their claims to absolute ultimate authority, it was

---

[2] R. Koser, 'Die Epochen der Absoluten Monarchie in der Neueren Geschichte', *Historische Zeitschrift*, 61 (1889), 246–87.

[3] Michel L'Héritier, 'Le despotisme éclairé, de Frédéric II à la Révolution', *Bulletin of the International Committee of Historical Sciences*, 9 (1937), 181–225.

[4] B. Behrens, 'Enlightened Despotism', *Historical Journal*, 18 (1975) 401–8; a less hostile view in her *Society, Government and the Enlightenment: The Experiences of Eighteenth-Century France and Prussia* (London, 1985).

difficult to point to any eighteenth-century monarch who truly ruled despotically, that is without restraint by laws; let alone without challenge by elite groups and institutions. How, for example, could the history of the British monarchy, hedged around with Parliamentary restrictions as it was, be related to the concept of absolutism? What was the value of any term which could not stretch to the reality of government in what was a major state? There were others who pointed out that the ICHS definition encapsulated an interpretation of the Enlightenment itself which was fast being discarded. As we saw in chapter 1, by the 1960s, it was increasingly difficult to see the Enlightenment as in any way a unitary phenomenon, dominated by a few, mainly French, 'great thinkers'. 'Enlightenment' was increasingly seen as different from state to state, region to region, and thus it followed that the relationship between government and the crucible of concerns and debates that made up Enlightenment, would also be different.

Another, and even more damaging criticism of the concept of 'Enlightened Despotism' or 'Absolutism' was that it offered no way to separate out what government actions were specifically due to Enlightenment concerns, and those which were rooted in much older ideologies such as neo-stoicism, or were responses dictated by the pure pursuit of advantage.

By the 1970s, scepticism both about the value of the label 'Enlightened Despotism', and about the possibility of adequately investigating the relationship between Enlightenment and government to which it referred, was at an all time high, and seemingly with good reason. But, as usual in historical scholarship, at the very moment of its entrenchment, such scepticism itself came under attack. The sceptics, it was said, had confused an inadequate and misleading label with a more complex and interesting reality. Discarding the labels should not mean however that no further interest be paid to the relationship between government, policies, debates and attitudes in the eighteenth century. Was it not, to say the least, unlikely that monarchs and their ministers could so effectively insulate themselves as to know *nothing* of the often heated debates about government and society raging outside their palaces and offices? If Enlightenment *was* of no concern to monarchs, why did so many, like Catherine of Russia, or Frederick II of Prussia, bother to maintain lengthy correspondences, and long and often troublesome personal and financial relationships with figures such as Diderot and Voltaire?

Many of these perceptions crystallised due to the publication and translation of work by Franco Venturi. His publication of numerous texts by Italian economists, historians and political commentators, many of whom were also governmental advisors, showed beyond a doubt the importance of Enlightenment ideas in the making of governmental policies and attitudes.[5] After this, a flurry of reconceptualisations emerged. It was suggested, for example, that Enlightenment could be understood as a facilitator for 'modernisation'; though problems with understanding what was meant by 'modernisation' seemed at once to reflect the current quandaries of development economics, and to take the focus off the problem of understanding Enlightenment in a broader sense.[6]

A second point of view came from Marxism, then at the height of its intellectual and political influence in western Europe. The Marxist approach essentially saw Enlightenment as irrelevant to absolutism, assuming that the former was an ideology of the bourgeoisie, while monarchy existed to bolster the interests of the 'feudal' aristocracy. Thus, in the Marxist view, eighteenth-century monarchies were faced with the impossible task of trying to reconcile irreconcilable interests, feudalism and capitalism, aristocracy and bourgeoisie. Enlightenment acted merely as an 'ideological superstructure' which was used to gloss over the ensuing contradictions of values and interests.[7] There are, of course, many problems with this approach. It is difficult to apply to the many monarchies whose states, particularly in eastern and central Europe, contained no significant numbers of *bourgeois*; conversely, it is very open to doubt whether the aristocracy of many states, particularly in western Europe, could be helpfully described as 'feudal' by the eighteenth century. Nor is it easy to endorse the Marxist assumption that social groups are only receptive to or influenced by programmes directly related to their objective economic interests. This approach also, by definition, has little to offer the many different republican states. Nor were 'aristocracy' and 'bourgeoisie' monolithic social groups, with completely unified attitudes towards 'Enlightenment'. To treat the Enlightenment as mere 'superstructure' is also to perpetuate (though for very different reasons) the distinction between deeds and thoughts, which was so central, paradoxically, to the older style of historiography of the Enlightenment.

Different again was the approach in Reinhard Koselleck's influential

---

[5] Franco Venturi, *Settecento riformatore* (Turin 1969–), now in vol. V, part I; and his *Utopia and Reform in the Enlightenment* (Cambridge, 1971).

[6] E.g., A.M. Wilson, 'The Philosophes in the Light of Present Day Theories of Modernization', *Studies on Voltaire and the Eighteenth-Century*, 48 (1967), 1893–1913; H.B. Applewhite and D.G. Levy, 'The Concept of Modernization and the French Enlightenment', *ibid.*, 74 (1971), 53–96.

[7] For example, Perry Anderson, *Lineages of the Absolute State* (London, 1974); Albert Soboul, introduction to Philippe Goujard (ed.), *L'Encyclopédie ou Dictionnaire raisonné des Sciences, des Arts et des Métiers: Textes Choisis* (Paris, 1952, 1976, 1984); Horst Möller, 'Die Interpretation der Aufklärung in der Marxistische–Leninistischen Geschichtsschreibung', *Zeitschrift für Historische Forschung*, 14 (1977), 438–72.

1956 *Critique and Crisis*.[8] This work sees the relationship between Enlightenment and the state as being determined by reaction against the religious conflicts of the sixteenth and seventeenth centuries. Reformation ideology had enabled individuals and groups to legitimate unlimited *critique* of monarchies and rulers of different faiths, thus producing an era of pervasive and long-lasting disorder in Europe. In the eighteenth century, Koselleck argues, ordered government was re-established by the ideals of at least limited religious toleration – which stopped some governments from claiming to operate as ethical agents – and even more by the support given to the idea that 'critique', with all its disruptive consequences, should be confined to the private sphere. This is an idea which is still very strong, as we have already seen, in Kant's essay on Enlightenment.

Koselleck argues, somewhat controversially, that this situation can be traced back to the writings of the English political theorist Thomas Hobbes (1588–1679), who, in the aftermath of England's own Civil War, had argued for the subordination of the claims of individual morality, or 'critique', to the requirements of the necessity for a strong political order. This, however, Koselleck argues, left no clear place for the increasing levels of exchange of ideas and the rise of 'public opinion'. Public opinion and its informal institutions such as Masonic Lodges, or its conceptualisations such as the 'Republic of Letters', became substitutes for real politics, and judged monarchs and the politically active by 'utopian' rather than practical standards. Koselleck charges that these utopian judgements were 'hypocritical' in that they were taken from a position of irresponsibility and without adequate realisation of the impact of unrestricted 'critique' on the crisis of the old order by the end of the century.

Koselleck's book, even though published as long ago as 1956, has recently enjoyed a revival, manifested in its numerous recent translations. But it has also sustained many damaging cuts from critics, who have pointed out that this view of the relationship between Enlightenment and government is overwhelmingly driven by the author's wish to account for the Cold War, which had divided his own country. On a less grandiose level of explanation, it has also been questioned whether Hobbes was really representative of the seventeenth-century crisis of 'critique'; whether Enlightenment rulers really thought of themselves as ruling by *raison d'état* rather than by Christian values; a major ruler like Maria Theresa of Austria, for example, would hardly fit this bill. Was Enlightenment 'critique' really always undertaken in conditions of utopian

[8] Reinhard Koselleck, *Critique and Crisis: Enlightenment and the Pathogenesis of Modern Society* (Oxford, New York and Hamburg, 1988); originally published as *Kritik und Krise. Eine Studie zur Pathogenese der bürgerlichen Welt* (Munich, 1956).

hypocrisy and irresponsibility? This seems to be directly contradicted by the view of the Italian Enlightenment emerging so forcefully from the pen of Franco Venturi.

From this welter of controversy about the nature and meaning of 'Enlightened Despotism' or 'Enlightened Absolutism', emerges one major question: why have historians experienced, for so long, such a high level of difficulty in discussing this theme? Part of the problem for the eighteenth century undoubtedly arose from the way in which the Enlightenment was itself early characterised as an autonomous body of thought, floating free of situation and circumstance. Formulations of 'Enlightenment' as the ancestor of modern liberalism, such as that by Peter Gay, also produced unreal expectations for the actions of eighteenth-century monarchs, who were castigated if they failed to fulfil nineteenth- and twentieth-century 'liberal' criteria through refusing to abandon warfare, or refusing to restructure their societies and economies completely by abolishing such key institutions as serfdom. The task today is to find a way of thinking about the relations between Enlightenment and monarchy in a way which is more dynamic, less anachronistic, and more sensitive to the pressure of regional and national patterns and situations.

Previous historiography thus seems to have hindered rather than helped our understanding of the relationship between government and Enlightenment. In any case we would encounter considerable difficulties in trying to approach this theme. Governments come in all shapes and sizes and face very different challenges. Large national states such as France were no less a part of Enlightenment Europe than were the merchant oligarchies of the Venetian and Genoese Republics. Giant multinational monarchies such as Austria and Russia co-existed with more than three hundred small German states. Clearly the challenges faced by large and small states, monarchies and Republics, were very different, as were their previous histories, and the local ideologies of what constituted good government. There is also the problem that all states in this period faced stresses which may have been heightened in the eighteenth century but which were still not different in kind from those faced by previous generations. The pressures of warfare and international competition, the problem of obtaining the cooperation of elites and ordinary people alike, the challenges of rising population and economic expansion, had all faced governments before.

In this sense eighteenth-century government was business as usual. It is also the case that many states particularly in central Europe already possessed a much older body of thinking about the nature, operation and legitimation of government, which remained powerful well into the

Enlightenment. This body of thinking was called Cameralism. Cameralism was particularly powerful in the German-speaking areas of Europe, in the Austrian monarchy and the German states, as well as in areas which often drew their governmental elites from Germany and Austria, areas such as Sweden, Denmark and Russia. So important was this body of thought that it might even be argued that one of the major divisions within Europe was not so much between Catholic and Protestant states, or large and small states but between states which used Cameralist thinking and those which did not.

France, so often seen as the heart of the Enlightenment, saw few of its leading intellectuals in office, or acting as close advisors to government. In spite of the growth of 'public opinion', power remained largely in the hands of the aristocracy, and the struggle to enter its ranks was fierce. Among the ruling class, there was little consensus on future directions for the monarchy, just as there was little consensus among the intellectuals. Few wished to challenge the existing order outright, but opinion was divided on whether the powers of the monarchy should be decreased (to avoid 'despotism'), or increased (to achieve reform, efficiency and greater equity, through restructurings of government, finance, and the army opposed by powerful entrenched interest groups). All this led to a lack of consistency in support for reforming ideas, and also prevented the adoption of efforts to create and teach a technical science of government on the model pursued in the German states. In spite of much support for Enlightenment, improvement and physiocracy among the intendants, the single appointment of a genuine Enlightenment intellectual in high office in central government, the physiocrat Anne-Robert Turgot (1727–81), was a disaster. Weakened from the start by wavering court support, Turgot had to be removed from office when his insistence on establishing a free market in grain led to massive price rises, and the violent resistance by ordinary people, which historians have labelled the 'Guerre des Farines' of 1775. Other reforming ministers with strong connections to the Physiocrats, were likewise briefly supported by the monarchy, then abandoned. In France 'Enlightenment', in the political sphere, often seemed to become merely grist to the mill of the competing court factions. It did not act as a unifying factor for the French upper class, even less so as in the 1770s conflict between the efforts of the King and his ministers to achieve reform, and the efforts of bodies like the Parlements to resist them in the name of the nation, became acute, and divided the French governing class.

Very different was the situation in the German states, and in the central government of the Habsburg lands. Here, a highly organised body of thought antedating the Enlightenment, called Cameralism, attempted to deal with the science of, and justification for, bureaucracy and monarchy. Cameralism emphasised the importance of a state's wealth, and empha- sised the virtues of a strong government in obtaining this objective.[9] Cameralism also argued that rulers should attempt to regulate the lives of their subjects in detail to obtain the vital economic objectives of a strong, healthy, numerous, and loyal population. Cameralism was important, because however much it emphasised the importance of the strong state, it also included social regulation and *social* welfare among the characteristic and legitimate objectives of government, not just the *dynastic* and personal aims with which rulers often approached war and territorial acquisition. It was thus a set of beliefs about government which were well adapted to the German situation where many states were too small to afford their rulers any stage for dynastic posturing; it also worked well in the Habsburg lands, where the challenge of the 1740s – rising aggression between Austria and Prussia, which led to the global war known as the War of the Austrian Succession – made successive rulers well aware of the importance of control and development if they were to muster the necessary resources to compete with predatory rivals such as the Prussia of Frederick II.

The replication of Cameralist thinking was institutionally assured by the foundation of a wave of new universities and training schools in the German states whose *curricula* were primarily geared toward the training of an enlightened, Cameralist bureaucracy often under the close super- vision of the monarchs themselves. This meant that, quite differently to the situation in France, university teachers often occupied major govern- ment positions, and the converse was also true.[10] All these factors helped to make sure that high-ranking bureaucrats became an international class, often moving from state to state. This itself helped to homogenise thinking about government, about the direction of reform programmes, and about social and economic intervention, across wide geographical areas.[11] This is why there was such relative homogeneity in government thinking across the areas affected by Cameralist thinking, which also

[9] 'A prince, ordered by God to be leader and protector of a people, is justified in doing everything that the welfare of the state entrusted to him demands', Joseph von Sonnenfels, *Politische Abhandlungen* (Vienna, 1777), 254. A.W. Small, *The Cameralists* (Chicago, 1909), is still useful. See also K. Tribe, 'Cameralism and the Science of Government', *Journal of Modern History*, 56 (1984), 263–84.

[10] E.g., Johann von Justi occupied the positions of Professor of Cameralism at Vienna and Göttingen, as well as being Director of Mines for Prussia.

[11] The impact of Cameralism on Russia is discussed in the classic study by Marc Raeff, *The Well-Ordered Police-State: Social and Institutional Change through Law in the Germanies and Russia 1600–1800* (New Haven, 1983); 'The well-ordered police state and the development of modernity in seventeenth and eighteenth-century Europe', *American Historical Review*, 80 (1975), 1221–43.

spread into modernising states like Russia. This was not to say that relations between Cameralism and rulers were always smooth: thinkers such as Joseph von Sonnenfels, sometimes produced ideas which were seen as pushing change too far. But it is still generally true that Cameralism acted, far more than did Enlightened attitudes in France, as a unifying factor between monarchs, their servants and their societies, and gave coherence to the governing elite itself.[12] Cameralism also had other impacts. While not anti-religious, it certainly placed great weight on a view of government, and hence monarchy itself, as a machine for producing action and decisions, rather than a location for sacred unifying symbolism. This is the importance of Justi's description, at the head of this chapter, of government as a machine – and machines are devices for turning work into output – and the monarch as only the supreme mechanic. Cameralism also saw the basis for the monarchy's responsibilities to its subjects as lying in natural law as much as in Christian dogma. Nature and economic life were both seen as open to 'management' and exploitation to meet the needs of the state, and justified by rationality. This is an important point, because it showed how in many ways Cameralism was congruent with central Enlightenment concerns such as the importance of 'rationality'. Such concerns also enabled governments to offer legitimation for intervention in society, a legitimation particularly important for those rulers whose territories, like those of the Austrian Habsburgs, included a multiplicity of local privileges and jurisdictions, capable of providing obstruction to the ruler.[13] Cameralism, for example, allowed the construction of a theoretical basis for proceeding with agrarian reform if necessary without the consent of the aristocracy, by reference to man's duty to control nature – thereby exhibiting rationality – and by the search for natural justice through uniform legal structures. The drive towards fuller exploitation of the resources of economy and nature, could often only be achieved by imposing a uniform relationship to the monarchy on regions with very different legal definitions of their obligations to the crown.

It is probably a misconceived enterprise to try to untangle the specifically Enlightenment contribution to Cameralism. It is probably more fruitful to adopt a 'functionalist' approach, and try to establish *how* the holding of such ideas about government helped or hindered rulers in their search for international success and internal stability and prosperity. One

---

[12] See, for example, the arguments of Rudolf Vierhaus, *Deutschland im 18 Jahrhundert: Politische Verfassung, Soziales Gefüge, Geistige Bewegungen* (Göttingen, 1987).

[13] For examples of legitimations produced for specific policies of reform in the Habsburg lands, see E. Wangermann, 'The Austrian Enlightenment', in R. Porter and M. Teich (eds.), *The Enlightenment in National Context* (Cambridge, 1981), 127–40, esp. 134.

8 Portrait of Friedrich Anton von Heynitz (1725–1802), director of
the *Bergakademie*, or state school of mines at Freiburg in Saxony.
Devastated by the Seven Years' War (1756–1763), the Saxon
monarchs initiated an ambitious reform programme in 1763. Heynitz
was persuaded to leave the services of the Duke of Brunswick, to head
state training in mining and metallurgy. The splendour of this
portrait, which shows Heynitz carrying the axe of office, and wearing
symbols of mining on his uniform, leaves us in no doubt as to the
value placed by the Saxon monarchy on technology and the
exploitation of nature as an integral part of reform programmes
necessitated by involvement in prolonged military conflict
characteristic of the eighteenth century.

could argue that legitimation for measures of social and economic reform, such as the reform of guild organisations to which the Austrian monarchy devoted much effort, gave governments wider choices in policy. Universalistic appeals to Enlightenment values such as humanitarianism, potentially gave princes a legitimate way to disregard particularism and local rights by appealing to the elites' sense of belonging to an enlightened section of society. In other ways, Enlightenment ideas could also actually limit the options open to government particularly in often ruling out the use of greater force against the peasantry in the cause of agricultural reform.[14] If reform continued at a moderate pace, as was the case under Maria Theresa of Austria (1740–80), appeals to Enlightenment values could disguise, or make it more difficult for educated elites to oppose, the increasing efforts by governments to exploit natural and economic resources in their territories in ways which directly competed with the exploitation of those same resources by the aristocracy and church. In some contexts, able to point to a compelling combination of injunctions generated by Enlightenment universalistic ideals, as well as the danger posed by external threats, monarchs were more able to persuade privileged groups in society to accept changes which enhanced the state. Monarchs, such as Frederick the Great were able to persuade their privileged orders to accept changes which enhanced the power of the state, by subsuming their own personal powers in that of the state apparatus. The privileged orders were inclined to accept the situation if they could see that the state was being run in their interests, as Prussia was, and Austria did not appear to be after 1780, and if the monarchy was particularly successful in warfare, as that of Prussia was and that of Austria was not. In doing so, in this particular way, monarchies were also often (though not always) able to decrease the 'transaction costs', or frictions in the machine of government. In this process, Cameralism succeeded in both providing continuity with the pre-Enlightenment period, and with paving the way for Enlightenment objectives.

It is now time to look at the impact of specific bodies of thought on the operation of government. We have already discussed in chapter 3 the importance of religious thinking to rulers. Movements of religious reform such as Pietism allowed rulers such as Frederick William I of Prussia to legitimise programmes of church reform in the monarchy's interest. Even without the appearance of such reform movements within the churches there would still have been very considerable unity within Enlightenment thought about the necessity for church reform. Jansenist concerns about

---

[14] John Komlos, 'Institutional Change under Pressure: Enlightened Government Policy in the Eighteenth-Century Habsburg Monarchy', *Journal of European Economic History*, 40 (1978), 234–51; Wangermann, 'The Austrian Enlightenment', 135–7.

returning to the simplicities of the early church fitted well with the concerns of governments struggling to diminish the power of the Catholic church within their own dominion, as is shown by the universal attack on the Jesuit order from 1759. Rulers like Joseph II attacked the church's hold over education by attempting to set up a system of secular schools, and by opening the University professoriate to laymen. Joseph like his brother Peter Leopold, legislated against ecclesiastical practices which were seen as a drain on economic productivity: excessive numbers of monks and nuns, of Saints' days holidays, excessive display in church services, interparochial processions that often became the occasion for competitive conspicuous consumption, not to mention scenes of wild disorder. Religious orders which did not perform socially useful functions such as teaching or nursing were forbidden to take in new recruits, and many religious houses were closed. In Tuscany, Peter Leopold used his Jansenist bishops to spearhead reductions in the power of the episcopate and the economic and social functions of the church. At the same time Joseph II began as we have already seen to increase toleration for non-Catholic groups. These religious measures were undertaken for a variety of motives. Motives ranged from the military (declining religious recruitment would increase the pool of recruits for the army), the economic (releasing church resources into more productive uses), the legal (enhancing the jurisdictional power of the monarchy at the expense of that of the church), the social (hoping to control disorderly behaviour associated with lavish and frequent church ceremonies) and last but not least by gaining control of education, of refocussing loyalty from Pope to monarch.

While Joseph II's methods were the most radical, most Catholic states adopted some version of this programme, showing a commitment to a quite uniform set of policies. At the same time there was also genuine commitment to a new religious value: that of toleration. While Frederick II experienced no serious opposition to his toleration policies, Joseph II had a thankless and politically damaging task in introducing toleration edicts in the Habsburg Monarchy. That Joseph persisted in his efforts to enhance toleration could only have been due to personal commitment. Toleration not only aroused hostility, it also hacked at the roots of the church–state relationship traditional to the Austrian Monarchy, and involved it implicitly in a radical redefinition of its own powers and legitimation, as we saw in chapter 3. It is first in the campaign for toleration that we see possibly most clearly demonstrated both the commitment of some monarchs to a specifically Enlightenment idea, and the price that they paid for it.

Many attempts to reform the structures of the church had strong economic motivations. In many Catholic countries the church was a major landowner, if not the largest single landowner. Economists such as Pietro Verri in Milan or Francesco Galiani in Naples pointed out that the church's dominance of the land market retarded agricultural development and prevented the emergence of a dynamic land market which could adjust to the needs of a rapidly rising rural population and generate higher agricultural profits. This attack on the church's economic role was only one aspect of economic debate in the Enlightenment much of which had direct impact on government. For most governments, especially in western Europe the Enlightenment saw the abandonment of previous orthodoxies which have usually been described under the collective heading of Mercantilism, and which, in general, held that real wealth lay in manufactures and in the accumulation of precious metals and restrictions on trade with commercial competitors. In the eighteenth century, as the economy expanded, it became more widely accepted that economic resources also included people, industry and innovation, and that free trade was likely to benefit all by making a generally higher level of economic activity possible. These ideas were developed by a group in France often known as the physiocrats, who saw the true basis of wealth as land and agriculture. They believed that wealth was dependent on free trade in agricultural products. Higher prices would lead to greater profits, profits would raise agricultural productivity, and greater abundance would be produced in the long run. Physiocrats, who included influential publicists such as Mercier de la Rivière, Quesnay, Mirabeau and Dupont de Nemours, advocated the end of government controls on grain, the abolition of internal custom barriers, and the end of monopolies in trade. For a brief period (1774–6) the Physiocrat Anne-Robert Turgot was in control of French government finances, and lifted government controls on grain, as Peter Leopold in Tuscany was also to do in this period. The results were predictable in both cases: a rapid rise in the price of grain, followed by widespread riots by the poor. In Turgot's case, the aptly named *Guerre des Farines* of 1775 produced such disturbances that it was directly responsible for the abandonment of free trade in grain, and the minister's own fall from power.

In the long run, far more influential were the economic theories of Adam Smith, who published his *Inquiry into the Nature and Causes of the Wealth of Nations* in 1776. Smith was convinced, unlike the physiocrats, of the importance of manufacturing industry. Smith emphasised the idea that what increased wealth was not agriculture or industry *per se*, but how *labour* was applied to human activity. Nature, or, alternatively, the operation of self-interest, would infallibly secure the deployment of labour where it was most productive. Smith's views were highly influential. But to put them into practice would have required that restrictive labour practices such as guild organisations should be weakened on the Continent to the extent that they already were in Britain. Governments which, like Austria for the 1740s, or France for the 1780s, tried to weaken guild organisation did so under heavy and effective fire from traditionalists. Nor did Smith's study of the division of labour really address the situation in eastern Europe, where industrialisation had barely begun, colonial trade, where it existed, was still carried out under heavy protectionist tariffs, and, above all, the majority of the labour force were unfree serfs. 'Enlightened' rulers such as Frederick II of Prussia, or Catherine of Russia, unlike Joseph II, did not actively seek to destroy serfdom. Joseph paid a very high price in terms of heavy resistance from aristocratic landlords in Hungary and Bohemia; Catherine and Frederick gained a generally harmonious relationship with their aristocratic elite from their abstention from the issue. In this area, as so often, the limits of Enlightenment were set by fear of social and political chaos.

It is thus easy to see that specific debates generated by the Enlightenment did have an effect on actual government policy. On a broader canvass, we can also say that Enlightenment did cause some fundamental questioning of the basis of monarchy, the most common form of government in eighteenth-century Europe. By the end of the century it is certainly possible even to discern a change in how monarchs thought of themselves. This is an important point to make, not simply by virtue of the radical challenge to monarchy in France after 1789, but also because in major and minor states alike, the implementation of Enlightenment policy, for all its rationality and universalism, was almost always still dependent on the physical survival, or the human will of the monarch. At any moment, long-term reform plans could be overturned by death or whim. This was something which happened for example, to Peter Leopold's policies in Tuscany, after his departure for Vienna in 1790. The ruler, his or her powers and his or her way of legitimating authority, was crucial for Enlightenment reforms. We have already seen (chapter 3) for example how Maria Theresa's self-image as a Catholic monarch, deriving legitimation from the church and from her membership of a community of believers, led her to adopt an attitude towards the issue of religious reform which was radically different from that of her son, Joseph II. By the end of the century, the religious legitimations of monarchical rule, the belief that monarchy in general, as well as each individual monarch, were chosen by God to rule as his lieutenants was becoming eroded, as was the elaborate court ceremonials evolved in the seventeenth century to emphasise the distance between monarchs and ordinary mortals. Louis XVI of France, Joseph II of Austria, and Frederick of

Prussia all dispensed with much of this ceremony. As Joseph said, he became more like a student than a conqueror. While Louis XVI certainly retained a vision of monarchy as divinely sanctioned, and legitimated by the Catholic church it was precisely this which was to bring him into the conflict with widespread opinion within the regime which ruled France after 1789.

If kingship itself was becoming secularised, it was also losing its 'proprietary' character. Few believed, as had Louis XIV, that their territories were theirs in the same way that ordinary men possessed personal property. It is difficult to avoid the conclusion that this change was helped by the way in which the Enlightenment had begun to reflect on what legitimate government might be. Often, the answer they arrived at did not look very much like traditional absolutism. Locke, for example, had opened the century with his *Two Treatises on Government*, with an argument that what constituted legitimate government was not divine right, but a contract between government and subjects. As the century progressed, the idea that human beings were innately locations of 'rights' which could not be overridden by governments also started to become more powerful, even though the application of demands for 'rights' beyond the boundaries of race and gender (chapters 5 and 6) were still seen as deeply problematic, and the notion of rights itself was thus not taken to its logical extension. All these tendencies led to monarchy being regarded in quite a different way. Enlightenment and the justification of 'despotism', the rule of one person without the restraint of legality or the subject's welfare, truly were incompatible. It was because of this that some Enlightenment princes, for example, Peter Leopold in Tuscany, and Frederick II in Prussia, began to draft constitutions which would make manifest the nature of the contract between ruler and ruled and stabilise it beyond the lifetime of a particular monarch.

Enlightenment ideas, like all ideas, cannot simply be understood in a functional sense. Their impact cannot be understood if we regard them merely as tools which enabled rulers to do with new and better legitimation that which external threat and international competition pressed them to do in any case. They were not simply grist to the mills of Justi's machine state. They were not simply means to an end (and means often alter ends). They carried messages of their own. Through these messages, perceptions about the nature of monarchy itself were to change dramatically in some parts of Europe by the end of the century, both for subjects and for the monarchs themselves.

Part of this change came from tensions inherent in the relationship between monarchy itself and programmes of Enlightened reform. Because of the supreme executive power still held by most European rulers, the fate of programmes of reform was still dependent on the decisions of the ruler, who could withdraw support from policies at a moment's notice. The death of a ruler, or his departure to rule other realms, could throw entire reform programmes into doubt, as occurred for example in Tuscany, when its Grand-Duke Peter Leopold departed to Vienna in 1790 to succeed his brother Joseph II as Emperor of Austria. Monarchal will, and monarchal mortality thus posed deep problems for officials and sections of the elites committed to reform programmes which only had validity as long-term enterprises. At a conceptual level, the premises of rationality and uniformity on which many Enlightenment and Cameralist policies were based, were at odds with the intrinsically personal nature of monarchal involvement.[15] Enlightenment also raised another problem: how far was 'critique', the use of rationality, to be allowed to proceed? Who was to be allowed to exercise this allegedly universal human trait, and to what extent? This is exactly the question raised by Kant's famous essay (chapter 1). Was not the untramelled exercise of reason sure to perturb that very authority on which the practical implementation of Enlightenment depended?

Was there any way out of these dilemmas, short of the path of revolution, of the overturning of monarchy and its replacement by the rule of the (allegedly) virtuous and rational elite in the name of the sovereign people, as was to occur in France? By the 1780s, it was officials in the German states who were trying to find a peaceful way out of this dilemma. They were helped in their reformulation of monarchy by the increasing tendencies of monarchs themselves to discard the ceremonial and symbolic aspects of kingship which their ancestors had expended such energy in creating. Louis XVI of France turning to artisan trades in his spare moments (one can hardly imagine Louis XIV patiently constructing watches and turning table legs) was only one among many, in an age which saw the disintegration of elaborate royal ceremonial and symbolism. Joseph II of Austria saw himself at moments as a bureaucrat compiling information, rather than as God's regent, as the opening quotation of this chapter shows. Frederick the Great encapsulated this process by describing himself as the 'First Servant of the State', a description which while in no way diminishing the King's absolute position in the state, did place the focus squarely on the monarch as justifying his position in terms of *deeds*, rather than by providing a sacralised symbolic centre for the realm. Other voices, more radical, called for princes to give written constitutions to their states, which would

---

[15] J. Mack Walker, 'Rights and Functions: The Social Categories of Eighteenth-Century Jurists and Cameralists', *Journal of Modern History*, 40 (1978), 234–51; Wangermann, 'The Austrian Enlightenment', 135–7.

stabilise the tension between princely will, and long-term reform programmes on universalistic, rational lines. The *Berliner Monatsschrift*
asked in 1785, only two years after the Constitution of the new American
State was introduced, for example, for a Constitution which would make
it impossible 'for his successors arbitrarily to alter the laws he had
introduced'.[16] Elements in the Prussian bureaucracy also put forward the
idea that in an absolutist state, it was they who stood in the place of a
constitution, as it was they who assured the continuity of the state; and
that their position should be protected by legal guarantees against
arbitrary decrees by the monarchy. Many of these ideas were encapsulated in the *Allgemeines Landrecht*, the first unified law code for Prussia,
debated under Frederick II and drawn up in 1794. At many points, the
Landrecht deliberately sets the state, as a permanent organisation, above
the mortal person of the monarch.

In conclusion: By the end of the century, most major states in Europe,
as well as many minor ones, were committed to programmes of reform
which often involved substantial modifications of interest groups, such as
trade guilds, sovereign legal bodies, aristocratic representative institutions and legal jurisdiction over their tenants, and often the economic and
jurisdictional interests of the Catholic church. These programmes also
involved steadily more intervention by the monarchies in the social life of
their subjects, by such means as programmes of public hygiene, setting up
of systems of elementary education, and economic regulation. These
programmes were designed to produce a healthy educated population,
capable of giving rational assent to monarchal measures. Many of these
programmes were set in motion by the pressure on all states to reform,
which came from the increased pressures of global competition. Many of
them represented major change, and were legitimated by Enlightenment
ideas such as benevolence, and the duties of states to produce rational
assent to policies through education.[17] None were aimed at producing
major increases in social mobility, or basic transfers of power in society.
These 'limits to reform' have often been discussed: the fact that Enlightenment rulers were reluctant to contemplate major and therefore
risky social upheaval, does not lessen their debt to the Enlightenment, few
of whose thinkers ever contemplated this either. But, in the end, Enlightenment was able to raise major problems for monarchies, as well as
being of major importance in reform. Its reform programmes pointed

---

[16] Quoted in F. Hartung, 'Enlightened Despotism', Historical Association Pamphlet,
London, 1957, 29. This article first appeared in *Historische Zeitschrift*, 180 (1955).
[17] James Van Horn Melton, *Absolutism and the Eighteenth-Century Origins of Compulsory
Schooling in Prussia and Austria* (Cambridge, 1988); Harvey Chisick, *The Limits of
Reform in the Enlightenment* (Princeton, 1981).

logically to a dissociation of the personal ends of the monarchy from the needs of the state, a situation which would have been an anathema to an earlier phase of Absolutism typified by 'L'état c'est moi'. Enlightenment also assisted in the creation of important new factors, such as 'public opinion', which intervened in the process of social and political manipulation by monarchies. Enlightenment gave subjects new aspirations and new expectations from monarchs, expectations for change and reform which were useful if successfully mobilised by monarchs, but were difficult to control in regimes without sufficient institutional representation of the unprivileged. Once 'critique' began, it was difficult to stop. In the end, Enlightenment and 'despotism' or absolute monarchal power, were difficult to reconcile. It is a measure of the success of many monarchs, paradoxically, in using Enlightenment to diminish the frictions of the machine of state that the conflicts between Enlightenment and monarchy started to become intense only late in the century. Whether the resulting *impasse* actually 'caused' the French Revolution and its associated upheavals is discussed in the final chapter of this book.

8   The end of the Enlightenment: conspiracy and revolution?

The empire of ignorance and superstition was moving closer and closer towards its collapse, the light of Aufklärung made more and more progress, and the convulsive gestures with which the creatures of the night howled at the dawning day showed clearly enough that they themselves despaired of victory, and were only summoning up their reserves for one final demented counter-attack. Then the disorders in France erupted: and now they again reared their empty heads and screeched at the top of their voices, 'Look there at the shocking results of the Aufklärung! Look there at the philosophers, the preachers of sedition!' Everyone seized this magnificent opportunity to spray their poison at the supporters of the Aufklärung.[1]

In 1789, France entered a period of revolutionary change which was to see the complete restructuring of the state, the collapse of the monarchy, and its replacement by a republic. By 1793, France was riven by civil war and factional struggles caused by these changes, and had also opened hostilities upon several neighbouring states. At home, political dissent and economic collapse were repressed by the use of political terror. For many contemporaries, as for later historians, the connection between these events and the Enlightenment was highly problematic. How could an era which had seen so much struggle for the rational reform of society, government and the individual, have ended with such turmoil and violence? Was the Revolution caused by the Enlightenment, or was it a repudiation of it? Did it happen because Enlightenment had been pursued too strongly or not strongly enough? Was Revolution always implicit in Enlightenment, or had the Revolution in France only occurred because of much more contingent, short-term factors? In particular, was the violence of the Revolution, which traumatised contemporaries, an inevitable outcome of the intense political stresses of a revolutionary situation after 1789, or was it generated by the ideas of the Enlighten-

---

[1] Quoted from the *Oberdeutsche Allgemeine Literaturzeitung* of August 1793, in T.C.W. Blanning, 'The Enlightenment in Catholic Germany', in R. Porter and M. Teich (eds.), *The Enlightenment in National Context* (Cambridge, 1981), 126.

ment, ideas in which the men of the Revolution were thoroughly steeped? The answers to these questions were to be of decisive importance in assessing the importance of both Enlightenment and the Revolution itself in the nineteenth century. In turn, this Revolution did much to shape public attitudes towards social change and revolutionary movements ever since. Conservative writers such as the influential French historian Henri Taine, interpreted the impact of the Enlightenment on the Revolution in very negative ways, ways which are therefore very different from the insistence upon Enlightenment as an uncompleted project of immensely liberating force, which is characteristic of the writings of some twentieth-century theorists such as Jürgen Habermas.

Possibly the best known of the conservative interpreters of the Enlightenment and its impact upon the French Revolution was the Abbé Barruel (1741–1820), a former Jesuit, whose 1797 *Mémoires pour servir à l'histoire du jacobinisme* was of great importance in determining many of the attitudes of the nineteenth century towards the Enlightenment and its links with the French Revolution. Barruel published his book in an atmosphere of political instability only to be ended with Bonaparte's seizure of power in 1799. As an ex-Jesuit he had also well-founded personal reasons for disliking the Enlightenment principles which had contributed to the downfall of his order, and his own consequent exile in Russia. Barruel believed that the Revolution in France, with all its attendant violence, and the sacrilege of its attack upon the French monarchy and the Catholic church in France, had been caused by a conspiracy of Enlightenment *philosophes*, banded together in secret organisations such as the Illuminati in Germany, or the Masonic lodges which had spread through many parts of Europe. While the writings of the *philosophes* undermined the traditional values on which state and society depended, members of the Illuminati or the habitués of the Masonic lodges infiltrated government. For Barruel it was clear that the French revolutionary political faction known as the Jacobins, during whose period of dominance the use of terror in the Revolution had peaked, were nothing more than the continuation of this conspiracy to destroy civil society. Barruel thus saw the Revolution not as a radically new form of politics, or a dramatic break with the past, as did many of the revolutionaries themselves, but much more as the unmasking of very long-term previous developments within the Enlightenment.

The detail of these arguments may seem absurd to us: conspiracy theories to explain grand historical developments have had a bad press in this century. Benefitting from more than a century's work on the origins and course of the Revolution, his thesis now seems unable to account for the diversity of factors which went into the making of the Revolution in

France, let alone to reflect the diversity of the Enlightenment itself. Some of Barruel's contemporaries, even those opposed to the Revolution in France, found his arguments unconvincing. But it is worth remembering that others did not. Barruel's arguments were for example foreshadowed in Edmund Burke's famous 1790 *Reflections on the Revolution in France*.[2] His work became a best-seller and had a widespread impact not simply on expert appraisals of the relationship between Enlightenment and Revolution, but also on much wider public perceptions of these issues. The reasons for this are two-fold. Firstly, at the time of its publication, Barruel's *Mémoires* fitted into a thesis about Enlightenment which had already been consistently argued in other quarters during the eighteenth century itself, in a whole sub-species of novels and contemporary comment. For example the very popular novel *Le comte de Valmont*, which went into seven editions between 1774 and 1785, described a conspiracy of *philosophes* to gain control of Europe.[3] The conservative journal the *Année Littéraire*, had consistently argued for the idea of a *philosophe* conspiracy as early as the 1770s. Part of the impetus for this viewpoint came from the fact that the editor of the *Année Littéraire*, Elie-Catherine Fréron, and many of its contributors, who included Barruel himself for a time, were Jesuits dispossessed by the abolition of their order in 1773. Fréron and his team played cleverly on contemporary concerns, by making direct parallels between the alleged *philosophe* 'conspiracy' against throne and altar, and Protestant 'heresy' associated in the minds of their readers with the period of religious civil war in France in the sixteenth and seventeenth centuries, a period which had seen not only chaos and civil strife, but also a great weakening of the authority of the monarchy in France. As one recent historian puts it, the concept of conspiracy emerges as 'a secularized form of the idea of heresy' in the *Année Littéraire*, which was probably the most widely read journal in eighteenth-century France.[4]

These arguments played to renewed religious intolerance in France, which peaked in the famous case of the Protestant Jean Calas, convicted in 1762 on flimsy evidence of the murder of his son. Calas' rehabilitation was

---

[2] Compare Edmund Burke, *Reflexions on the Revolution in France*, ed. Conor Cruise O'Brien (London, 1986), 211: 'The literary cabal had some years ago formed something like a regular plan for the destruction of the Christian religion. This object they pursued with a degree of zeal which hitherto had been discovered only in the propagators of some system of piety.' For an opposing view see the royalist Mallet du Pan, 'Of the Degree of Influence which the French Philosophy has had upon the Revolution', *The British Mercury*, 14 (15 March 1799).

[3] Philippe-Louis Gérard, *Le comte de Valmont, ou les égarements de la raison* (Paris, 1774), which achieved twelve editions by 1807.

[4] Amos Hoffman, 'The Origins of the Theory of the *Philosophe* Conspiracy', *French History*, 2 (1988), 152–72.

the subject of a famous campaign by the atheist Voltaire. The success with which Fréron's band of writers played to such concerns should remind us of the extent to which religious issues still organised the thought of educated elites in Enlightenment France. It should also remind us that 'marginal' or 'dispossessed' men, as were Jesuits after 1773, making a living by the pen, did not always, as Robert Darnton would have us believe, devote their talents to attacking the powers that be. 'Grub Street' and the *Année Littéraire* were not ideological equivalents, and did not put out the same message.

Thus, by describing the Enlightenment as a form of heresy which wished to weaken throne and altar in the same way that Protestant theological 'heresy' had allegedly done in previous centuries, the *Année Littéraire* picked up on a whole series of concerns still vibrant in France in the eighteenth century. Such concerns were undoubtedly strong enough to raise support for Barruel's thesis by the 1790s and 1800s. By the 1820s, renewed evidence seemed to be on hand to support his arguments. The wave of revolutionary movements which swept through Europe in the 1820s and 1830s, and which were in fact, especially in southern European states such as Naples, influenced by secret societies of political activists, seemed to provide vivid empirical evidence of the link between conspiracy, revolution, and mutant forms of 'Jacobinism'.[5]

However, Barruel's was far from being the only attempt to ponder on the connection between Enlightenment and Revolution. In 1856, Alexis de Tocqueville published his *The Ancien Régime and the French Revolution*. De Tocqueville, a liberal politician worried by increasingly authoritarian trends in France after Louis Napoleon's seizure of power in 1852, was no conservative figure looking back with regret to a time when throne and altar stood unchallenged. He was strongly concerned to argue that there was a continuity between the eighteenth century and the Revolution, but he saw that continuity not as lying, as Barruel had argued, in a successful *philosophe* conspiracy, but rather in the increasing power of the centralised state, which had, he believed continued unabated between Old Regime and Revolution, and which had a capacity to extinguish true liberty, as much as had the excesses of mob rule. He argued that once catapulted into practical politics after 1789, the *philosophes*, whom he viewed as inexperienced utopian thinkers, had been unable to provide any ideological bulwark against the progress of political terror which had carried on the progress of centralisation. In fact their utopian idealism both before and after 1789 had created a situation where debate and

[5] See J.M. Roberts, *The Mythology of the Secret Societies* (Oxford, 1972); 'The French Origins of the "Right"', *Transactions of the Royal Historical Society*, 23 (1973), 27–53.

legitimate differences could not be contained, and terror became therefore the only way to exercise power, leading to a vast increase in dictatorial central government. For our purposes, De Tocqueville's influential history emerges as a negative version of Barruel's thesis.

Much of De Tocqueville's thesis has found echoes, some more distant than others, in current historical scholarship. Robert Darnton's emphasis on the oppositional writings of 'Grub Street' as a factor undermining authority at the end of the eighteenth century, is one example. So, in a different direction, is Keith Baker's thesis that the Republic of Letters served not only as a substitute for true political debate before the Revolution, but also as the prototype for the politics of the revolutionary public sphere.[6] Baker would agree with De Tocqueville that under the Old Regime

the philosophe's cloak provided safe cover for the passions of the day, and political ferment was canalised into literature, the result being that our writers now became leaders of public opinion, and played for a while the part which normally in free countries, falls to the professional politician.[7]

This opinion also converges with that in Habermas' arguments on the Enlightenment public sphere, which we examined in chapter 1. François Furet's recent re-interpretation of the Revolution also picks up this 'benign version' of De Tocqueville's thesis, by emphasising the importance of pre-revolutionary informal intellectual gatherings, the '*sociétés de pensée*', as foreshadowing many of the forms of revolutionary organisation and mobilisation.[8] All these modern interpretations, however, differ from that of De Tocqueville in one important respect. They are far more concerned with the *form* of association amongst *hommes de lettres*, *philosophes*, or amateur intellectuals, than in the actual *content* of the criticism of the Old Regime. In other words, they do not directly engage either with Barruel's accusations that the anti-regime *content* of their thought also damaged church and monarchy, or with De Tocqueville's accusations of impracticality or 'utopianism'. François Furet in particular makes little attempt to link his account of the specific nature of revol-

---

[6] K.M. Baker, 'Enlightenment and Revolution in France: Old Problems, Renewed Approaches', *Journal of Modern History*, 53 (1981), 281–303; 'In a critical conceptual shift, "opinion" became an imaginary substitute for "power" as symbolically constituted under the Old Regime, and took on some of its fundamental characteristics' (285).

[7] Alexis de Tocqueville, *The Old Regime and the French Revolution*, ed. H. Brogan (London, 1966), 163–64.

[8] François Furet, *Interpreting the French Revolution* (Cambridge, 1981) first published as *Penser la Révolution français* (Paris, 1978). Particularly relevant here is Furet's analysis of work by that 'most misunderstood among the historians of the French Revolution' (p. 212), Augustin Cochin, on what he calls the *sociétés de pensée* of the Old Regime, the heterogenous group of intellectual associations, ranging from provincial academies to masonic lodges and clubs.

utionary, especially Jacobin, thought and language, with that of the Enlightenment. Thus, emphasis on the continuity between the social forms of the Republic of Letters, and the political forms of the Revolution, leaves unanswered the question of the impact of the actual writings of the *philosophes*.

In part, this is a deliberate turning away from the style of analysis of for example, Louis Blanc, who in his 1847 *Histoire de la Révolution Française* makes a sustained attempt to trace the ideas of the *Encyclopédie* throughout the Revolution. It also reflects the fact that it is extremely difficult to assess the impact of Enlightenment writers on the Revolution, especially since the *philosophes* hardly produced a unified body of thought. While the revolutionaries themselves often alluded especially to Voltaire and Rousseau, their own thinking often proceeded in directions which would have horrified those whose names they used in order to legitimate their actions. It is debatable for example, whether Rousseau would have appreciated the uses to which his *Contrat Social* was put to justify the use of terror by reference to the General Will. While much use was made of appeals to Enlightenment ideals such as 'progress' or 'reason', few could foresee in 1789 the extent of the changes that were to occur by 1792. If the Enlightenment was not a unity, neither was the Revolution. To many it seemed that 1792 marked the opening of far greater changes than could have been thought of in 1789, and many subsequent historians have asked whether the years 1789–99 saw one Revolution or many separate ones, each with a different relationship to the eighteenth century and its own complex debates.

We are thus left with many unanswered problems, in our understanding of the relationship between Enlightenment and Revolution. Part of the problem stems from the great redefinition which has taken place in our understanding of the Enlightenment itself. It is no longer possible to see it, even within France itself, as a movement uniquely dedicated to the ideological undermining of throne and altar. Outside France, as we have seen (chapter 7), such an interpretation would have even less justification. At the same time, our understanding of the character of the Revolution itself has also greatly changed. Thanks to the work of François Furet and others, the French Revolution has ceased to be viewed, as Marxist orthodoxy would have it, as an episode of class struggle, and has increasingly been seen as a political phenomenon, driven by a particular political culture and discourse, whose origins in the Enlightenment are still unclear. Problems of chronology are also largely unresolved. Some historians, such as Dale Van Kley, have pointed out that the key words of the political discourse of the French Revolution, such as 'nation' or 'representation', had already been used as early as the 1760s by the

French Parlements, not in support of Enlightenment, but in their *opposition* to attempts by the Crown itself to change political and economic structures underpinned by tax inequality and privilege.[9] If the key terms of the Revolution's political discourse were in place so early, and if the Revolution can be understood as a phenomenon primarily of political culture, why did it take more than thirty years from the emergence of the key words of the Revolution, to the beginning of the collapse of the Old Regime? François Furet, on the other hand, seems to argue that the particular political culture of the Revolution crystallised very late, maybe as late as the election campaign for the Estates-General in 1788. Though we know a great deal more than we did before, therefore, on the nature of political culture in the Enlightenment, especially in France, it seems that, as each field is redefined, answers seem to be further away than ever.

Part of the problem might, however, lie in the linear approach which has been adopted in the debate. 'The Revolution' has been seen as the terminus of 'The Enlightenment'. This was particularly so, during the historiographical era which defined the Enlightenment as a peculiarly French phenomenon. Yet, anyone who looks at the course of the eighteenth century as a whole, can easily see that this is a misleading view. A peaceful period called 'Enlightenment', was *not* ended by a sudden upheaval called 'Revolution'. For most of Europe it is far truer to say that Enlightenment and Revolution proceeded side by side for much of the century. One could even say that the Enlightenment *began* with Revolution, that which occurred in England in 1688, which created the conditions for the emergence of the philosophy with which John Locke discussed new thinking about the relationship between ruler and ruled. Revolts against established authority, especially in the second half of the century, were widespread. From the 1760s onwards, the century saw revolts in places as far apart as Geneva (1764), Corsica, for which Rousseau produced a new draft Constitution (1720s and 1760s), the British colonies in North America (1775–83), and the Austrian Netherlands (1789). To these revolts Palmer has applied the term 'democratic'.[10] However this typology has aroused great controversy over *how* 'revolutionary' or democratic were the upheavals he chronicles. The Austrian Netherlands, for example, were as much concerned to restore the historical relationship of the province to Vienna which they saw as

---

[9] Dale Van Kley, *The Damiens Affair and the Unravelling of the Ancien Regime, 1750–1770* (Princeton, 1984) and 'The Jansenist Constitutional Legacy in The French Revolution', in K.M. Baker (ed.), *The French Revolution and the Creation of Modern Political Culture* (Oxford, 1987), I, 169–201.

[10] R.R. Palmer, *The Age of the Democratic Revolution* (2 vols., Princeton, 1956).

threatened by Joseph II, as they were to create a slight extension of political participation.

In this context, the American Revolution has often been seen as the place where Enlightenment ideas and a violent change of government can best be seen in conjunction. Certainly, the Americans did seem to want to create a '*novus ordo saeculorum*', a new order in the new world, not a return to a superior past. But how far can in fact the American colonists be seen as inspired by purely Enlightenment ideas in their struggle against British rule? It is certain that there are plenty of reasons for resentment between colony and home government even without any input from the Enlightenment. After 1763 London attempted to transfer the rising costs of empire, and the colossal war debt accumulated since 1754, to the colonies. This meant that the political relationship between the thirteen colonies and London came under increasing pressure, as the colonies questioned their lack of representation in the London Parliament which was laying such heavy new burdens upon them.

But the ideology that filled this conflict had many different sources. Puritan religious ideas of man's essential sinfulness sat uneasily with Enlightenment ideas of progress, optimism and faith in man's rationality and was strongly present in the colonies due to the religious revivals or 'Great Awakening' of the 1730s and 1740s. Other elements in American ideology also antedated the Enlightenment, especially the Republicanism which originated with classical models and was strengthened by the influence of the civic humanists of the Renaissance. The American interpretation of Republicanism emphasised the virtue of a simple society of autonomous citizens committed to the common good and emphasised the independence of each individual. While there was much here that would have appealed also to Rousseau, American ideals antedated those of the Genevan by many years. However Americans also believed that citizen and government should be united by contract, an idea very strong in John Locke's *Two Treatises of Civil Government*, which many have seen as the true opening of the Enlightenment itself. This idea of contract itself however ran into several difficulties in the American situation. Locke's idea of contract presupposed a society whose members were equal. Could it really be applied in the American colonies, which were underpinned by the labour of slaves? This is one of the central conflicts in the Enlightenment, and we have seen how difficult it was for the men of the Enlightenment, even for those not living in slave societies, to extend the logical implications of equality and natural rights to all those they classified as 'other' (see chapters 5, 6 and 7). Perhaps just because the American revolutionaries did try and create a *novus ordo*, they were bound to exemplify the ultimate problems of Enlightenment ideas in relation to change. Maybe in the end the American revolutionaries found themselves faced with the same problem as was to face the French twenty years later which was the impossibility of constructing a political order based on equality of rights without recasting the unequal social order. What the American Revolution perhaps teaches us is that some strands of the Enlightenment were powerful in allowing certain groups to think of change; but also that they could not overcome the limits to change which they envisaged as possible for the social order. This contradiction between support for supposedly universal rights, and the actual exclusion of large numbers of human beings from the enjoyment of those rights, is central to, and characteristic of Enlightenment thought.[11]

It is clear from our reflections on the American example that we obscure more problems than we solve if we think of the connection between 'Enlightenment' and 'Revolution' as meaning the French Revolution alone. It must also not be forgotten that not only did the eighteenth-century before 1789 see many attempts to change governments, but that it was also the case that the 1790s saw many other violent attempts in other countries outside France to change either the direction of government policy, or the actual holders of power. Many of these revolts were concerned quite explicitly with conflicts over Enlightenment programmes in government and they could be led by either opponents *or* supporters of Enlightenment. In Tuscany for example, a whole series of revolts broke out after the departure to Vienna of the Grand-Duke Peter Leopold, who succeeded his brother Joseph as Austrian Emperor. These so-called '*Viva Maria*' riots, as their slogan indicates, were triggered by opposition to religious reforms instituted by Peter Leopold and 'Jansenist' bishops in Tuscany, with the objective of reducing the splendour and extravagance of worship, the number of religious holidays, and the wealth of the religious orders, especially those who did no socially useful work.[12] In Hungary rebellion threatened over Emperor Joseph's own efforts to change relations between serf and landlord and to alter the relationship between Vienna and Budapest. Many rulers themselves back tracked away from Enlightenment reforming programmes in the 1790s, leaving isolated those elements in the elites and in the state service who had supported such reforms before. Such groups were the basis of French support in many areas when the armies of the French Revolution began to

---

[11] Henry F. May, *Enlightenment in America* (New York 1976); Colin Bonwick, *The American Revolution* (London, 1991); J.G.A. Pococke, *The Machiavellian moment: Florentine Political Thought and the Atlantic Republican Tradition* (Princeton, 1975).

[12] These riots soon also became linked to hostility to Peter Leopold's economic reforms, especially the deregulation of the grain trade. See Gabriele Turi, '*Viva Maria*': *La reazione alle riforme leopoldine 1790–1799* (Florence, 1969).

create satellite republics in the Netherlands, Switzerland, Naples, and Northern Italy after 1792; many in these areas managed to convince themselves that annexation by France was the only way to preserve Enlightenment programmes of reform. These contemporaries at least saw no break between Enlightenment and Revolution in France. That their hopes in the French were often partly or totally misplaced does not alter this fact. All this means that once we abandon the linear model of an older historiography, of an enlightened century ending catastrophically in revolution, we can thus see that the relationship between the two was far more complex. Revolt and revolution occurred throughout the Enlightenment. Some of it was accepted into the heart of the Enlightenment itself, which was evidenced by the lionising of Pasquale Paoli, the leader of the movement for Corsican independence from the Genoese Republic, who appeared as a heroic fighter against despotism to such diverse thinkers as David Hume and Jean-Jacques Rousseau. Others, like the '*Viva Maria*' uprisings in Tuscany, were in outright opposition to Enlightenment programmes.

Nor was the Enlightenment entirely at ease itself with the concept of 'revolution'. It is clear, for example, that it was only gradually in the eighteenth century that the word came to take on its twentieth-century connotations; thus, in asking about the link between Enlightenment and revolution, one is in danger of imposing anachronistic terminology, and thus defining a problem in a way unrecognisable to contemporaries. For much of the eighteenth century, it would seem from the evidence of dictionaries, and surveys of current usage, that 'revolution' derived its original meaning from mechanics and astronomy, and simply meant 'turning full circle' or 'a completed orbit', as in the phrase 'the earth's revolution around the sun'. In the context of political commentary 'revolution', especially in the early part of the century, meant a 'change bringing back a former state of affairs'. This fits in very well with the stated aims of the majority of 'revolutions' before 1776, which was to restore an original, and better, state of affairs, rather than to create a radically new one. As the century progressed, 'revolution' came to mean any upset of established order, any set of crises or changes. This is the way the term was used in the many history books published in the eighteenth century which had titles like 'The Revolutions of Poland' or the 'Revolutions of France'. The term 'revolution' only started to approach its modern meaning after the revolt of the American colonies against British rule which began in 1775. This successful revolt seemed to demonstrate to many contemporaries that it was possible to establish a new sort of state, a secular republic. This impression was enhanced when the thirteen colonies took as the motto of their federal seal, the words *Novus ordo saeculorum*, 'a new order of the centuries'. These words signified that this Revolution, far from restoring a former state of affairs, in fact, had created something completely new, a break in the passage of history, and a 'new order'. This was the sense of 'revolution' which was to be picked up by the French in 1789, and by all subsequent movements for change.[13]

It may be that historians have taken on board only the late-Enlightenment meaning of 'revolution', which makes problematic the links between Enlightenment and revolution by its assertion of the possibility of producing a political order radically different from that which has gone before, and have engaged too little with the problem of *how much* and what sort of change Enlightenment thinkers themselves saw as coming within the scope of their idea of revolution. Certainly, as the century progressed, an idea that human affairs manifested 'progress', rather than a series of reconstitutions of past affairs, began to come to the fore. The dominant metaphor for historical change, in other words, became 'time's arrow', rather than 'fortune's wheel', the metaphor so beloved by the Middle Ages and the Renaissance, became directional rather than cyclical. Thus at least some of the pre-conditions for being able to visualise radical distancing from the past were certainly present by the end of the Enlightenment, and due to classically Enlightenment ideas, such as that of 'progress'. That this process was far from complete, however, is shown by the way in which the Revolution in France, particularly in its Jacobin phase, produced a rhetoric which described itself *both* as a *return* to a Golden Age, and a new order of being, a total *break* with the preceding historical process.

However, Enlightenment thinkers were never far from the problem which as we have seen, was at the heart of Kant's *Essay on Enlightenment*: how far, and with what consequences, should ideas be allowed to achieve their full potential to effect change in the world? Most thinkers in France, as we have already seen, were clear that they did not want Enlightenment to percolate too far down the social scale, for fear of causing social upheaval. Those areas of central Europe which saw Enlightenment consciously used to foster and legitimate social change, did so in the context of the overall aim of the long-term stabilisation of society and monarchy. Educational policy in the Austrian lands, for example, was a matter of producing a less superstitious, more 'rational', hence more stable, acceptance by individuals, of the duties attached to the social status in which they were born, rather than aiding their social mobility.

It would thus seem that the dossier on the relationship between

---

[13] For fuller discussion of the word see K.M. Baker, *Inventing the French Revolution: Essays on French Political Culture in the Eighteenth Century* (Cambridge, 1990), 203–23.

Enlightenment and revolution, is still open. It is no longer possible to see Enlightenment simply as a movement of ideas located in France which produced a violent revolution there, either by reforming too much, or questioning too much, or, alternatively, by substituting opinion for politics to such an extent that needed reforms could only be carried out by revolutionary and violent means. Nor, in spite of the work of Darnton and others, is it possible to endorse fully arguments also common in the nineteenth century, that reading the works of the *philosophes* must necessarily have undermined the social and ideological consensus on which monarchy rested. It is difficult to argue about any given book, that its readers would be instantly mobilised to rise up against the powers that be. It is also right to stress that readers do not pick up a single unequivocal message from what they read. Every written message may be interpreted in many different ways by readers, some, if not many of them, unintended by the author. It is also probable that the growing circulation of books and pamphlets of a critical tendency, ranging from the pornographic attacks on the royal family, currently attracting notice in feminist scholarship[14] to serious commentary by Voltaire, Rousseau or Raynal, may partly only be the register or *result* of a pre-existing state of affairs, rather than its *cause*. The actual political and financial problems of the monarchy in France, its declining power to impress and mobilise elites, the attrition of the power of court life and royal patronage to mobilise the symbols of a powerful Christian monarchy, may have been the pre-conditions for the rise of Enlightenment critiques, rather than their result. All of which having been said, it is impossible to doubt that a rising tide of criticism of monarchy could hardly have failed to weaken its hold on the hearts and minds of subjects. Especially important here, at least in France, was the continual attacks on religious belief, belief on which the ideological foundations of the monarchy rested, and of which Louis XVI's own actions after 1789 show him to have been well aware. It is, however, quite another question as to whether, if Enlightenment contributed to revolution in France by weakening attachment, especially among the elites, for throne and altar, its influence necessarily caused the violence of the Jacobin phase of the Revolution, a phase which the majority of nineteenth-century commentators saw as the heart of the revolutionary experience. Beyond that question lies yet another which is still far from resolved: was the French Revolution a single movement, or several distinct revolutionary phases? That *dossier* too is still open.

More recently, Reinhard Kosselleck has argued in his *Critique and*

---

[14] E.g., Lynn Hunt, *The Family Romance of the French Revolution* (Berkeley, Los Angeles and London, 1992); *The Invention of Pornography* (New York, 1993).

Crisis that it was the internal contradictions of Enlightenment in central Europe and particularly in Prussia, which led to the creation of a revolutionary situation.[15] Whilst attempting reform, as we have seen, in accordance with some specifically Enlightenment ideals, such as rationality and uniformity (chapters 3 and 7) monarchs had still continued to insist on their positions guaranteed by dynastic right, and religious sanction. At the same time, many monarchs, especially Joseph II and Frederick the Great, dismantled a great deal of the court ceremonial which had been built up by their forebears with the objective of creating a symbolic order focussed upon the royal person. Tradition and innovation, rationality, universalism and the personal interventions of the monarch, uneasily combined, and, Kosselleck argues, produced a situation where contradiction had become so great as to paralyse the development of monarchy, so that further change and reform could not be achieved except by dismantling the basis of monarchy itself. This thesis also receives support from some contemporary comments. On the other hand, this case is also not proven. Who knows what would have happened had the outbreak of Revolution in France not led to a feeling of general instability in Europe which undermined reform programmes? It is also not impossible that monarchies themselves could have continued to evolve in the same direction, gradually bridging the contradiction between their traditional and sacral basis and their rationalist reform programmes. Kosselleck's argument, in other words, is posed in terms that make it impossible to answer. Nor should the extent of social opposition to Enlightenment reforms be forgotten. The 'Viva Maria' risings in Tuscany, the urban revolts in the Austrian Netherlands in 1789, and landlord resistance, coming very close to armed rebellion in Hungary, all show that far from ending in revolution because it was the only way out for Enlightenment policies at an *impasse* with the traditional basis of the old regime, it might be more that Enlightenment in central Europe ended in very much more traditional revolts aimed *against* enlightened policies and *for* the restoration of a previous state of affairs.

To sum up, much of the argument about the relationship between Enlightenment and revolution grew out of a historiography mesmerised by the Revolution in France, and in particular by its most violent, 'Jacobin' phase between 1792 and 1794. It failed to take account of the *concurrency* of Enlightenment and revolution in Europe and in the North American colonies of Britain. The limits of change and *critique* were constantly being tested within the Enlightenment itself. It also failed

---

[15] Reinhard Kosselleck, *Critique and Crisis: Enlightenment and the Pathogenesis of Modern Society* (Oxford, New York and Hamburg, 1988).

sufficiently to emphasise the difference in the practice and direction of Enlightenment in different regions of Europe, and played down the number of revolts at the end of the century which were not 'frustrated Enlightenments', as Kosselleck argues, or 'Enlightenments turning into revolutionary terror' as right wing historians would have argued, but were actual movements *against* Enlightenment policies by significant sections of society.

In the end, perhaps we may argue that Enlightenment posed no significant barrier in France, and in other states, to a mounting tide of criticism of the *status quo*, much of it from within the ruling class itself. Criticism of the powers that be of course was no new experience in European history. But what the Enlightenment had contributed was not only a great number of new, non-traditional ways of defining and legitimating power, through ideas such as 'natural law', 'reason', and so on, it had also mobilised sections of society into 'public opinion', which Kant had earlier identified as requiring tight control if it were not to disrupt social and political order. As remarked in chapter 2, the Enlightenment was much better at creating new relationships amongst elites, and bringing sections of elites together in the new forms of sociability centering on ideas, than it was in reaching out to lower social classes. Perhaps it was in this redefinition and remobilisation of elites, and their relationship with traditional sources of power, as well as in the specific nature of the ideas it discussed, that the Enlightenment in creating 'public opinion' also created conditions which given the right factors or political stress allowed revolution to occur. In the end, Kant's concerns about the disruptive impact of Enlightenment, a problem which has been at the heart of the concerns of this book, were probably justified.

Brief Biographies

1 Alembert, Jean le Rond dit d' (1717–83). Illegitimate son of the writer and *salon* hostess Claudine de Tencin (1682–1749) and rapidly famous as a mathematician. He was a member of the *salons* of Mme Geoffrin and Madame du Deffand, where he encountered his life-long passion, Julie de Lespinasse. With Diderot, he co-edited the *Encyclopédie*, and wrote its *Preliminary Discourse*, an important reflection on the nature and organisation of knowledge. He wrote about 1,400 articles for the *Encyclopédie*, which led him into controversy with Rousseau and the musician Rameau. After 1758, he allowed Diderot to take over the *Encyclopédie*, and began to write musical and literary criticism. In 1779 he became Perpetual Secretary of the Royal Academy of Sciences in Paris. D'Alembert has often been seen as one of the last thinkers capable of contributing over the whole range of knowledge.

2 Beccaria, Cesare (1738–94) is best known as the author of the Treatise *Dei Delitti e dei Pene* (1764), which had a huge impact on Enlightenment thinking on law, crime and capital punishment, which is denounced in his work, along with judicial torture and arbitrary justice. His book secularised the idea of punishment, which he argued was a necessary self-defence mechanism by the social structure, rather than an infliction legitimated by Divine sanctions against sin. His work left little indication as to how governments were to be persuaded to alter systems of criminal law; however, it was widely translated and did have a major impact, on practice, especially in the smaller states, such as Tuscany, and even in France, where judicial torture began to be dismantled in the 1780s.

3 Buffon, Georges-Louis Leclerc, Comte de (1707–88), was born at Montbard, of a family of high-ranking legal officeholders. After an important tour of Italy, took up residence in Paris, and was a member of both the *Académie française* and the Academy of Sciences. His impact on the Enlightenment stemmed primarily from his writings on natural history (*Histoire naturelle, générale et particulière*, 15 vols., 1749–67). Buffon saw nature as having a history far older than that suggested by Biblical chronology, and came close to supporting the idea that species could change over time. These views, and his implicit support for the idea that man was intrinsically *within* the natural order led to condemnations by the theology faculty of Paris in 1749. As Director of the Jardin Royal or botanical gardens, Buffon also played an important role in increasing the accessibility of natural history to the general public.

4 Catherine II (1729–96) Empress of Russia (1762–96), was influenced by Voltaire, Montesquieu and the *Encyclopédie*, and corresponded with Voltaire, Diderot, and with the salon hostess Mme Geoffrin. Tried to Europeanise Russia, but her relationship with the Enlightenment has often been questioned, as she systematically advantaged the nobility, and steadily increased the numbers of serfs. Her territorial conquests at the expense of Turkey and Poland also seemed to have had little to do with the general Enlightenment support for peaceful international relations. Nonetheless, her reputation was high amongst the *philosophes*, and Diderot resided for a short time at her court but quickly became disenchanted. Catherine was probably most influenced by Enlightenment thinkers on her project for a general law code for Russia.

5 Diderot, Denis (1713–84) achieved fame in his lifetime largely as the co-editor of the *Encyclopédie*, and to a lesser extent as a play writer, art critic and commentator on current issues – and of course none of these functions was wholly distinct. Many other works were known only posthumously, such as the *Supplément au Voyage de Bougainville*, published in 1796. Diderot came from a family of provincial artisans and work-shop owners, orthodox believers who saw their son take minor orders in 1726. Rejecting the religious life he earned a living as a lawyer's clerk, writer and private tutor, until his marriage in 1743. Diderot quickly rejected belief in the existence of a personal God, and instead saw nature itself and matter as full of energies, constantly in transformation. In apparent contradiction to this implicit determinism, Diderot also preached a secular morality of benevolence and civic virtue, as well as satirising what he regarded as social prejudices against adultery and sexual repression. In 1773–4 he visited Russia at the invitation of the Empress Catherine, but left disillusioned. Much of Diderot's ideas were also discussed in his extensive correspondence.

6 Frederick II, King of Prussia (1712–86). After a difficult early life, succeeded his father as King in 1740; in this year he seized the rich province of Silesia from Austria, and thus plunged Europe into the War of the Austrian Succession. In 1756, his aggression again triggered the international conflict known as the Seven Years' War. He played a leading role in the partition of Poland in 1773. During his reign, the Prussian economy was modernised, while the powers of the aristocratic class increased, and serfdom remained. Frederick surrounded himself with *philosophes* such as La Mettrie, the Marquis d'Argens and Maupertuis, whom he engaged to head the new Academy of Sciences in Berlin. Voltaire visited him in 1750. Frederick himself wrote extensively on his own life and times, and more generally on politics and kingship, pieces which were admired by the *philosophe* Grimm, and condemned by Diderot, in his 1771 *Pages contre un tyran*.

7 Herder, Johann Gottfried von (1744–1803) was born in East Prussia, of a strongly Pietist family, and became a pupil of Immanuel Kant at the University at Königsberg. Ordained in 1767, he took up a living in Riga, and published his *Fragments on a New German Literature*, where he argued for an independent German literature. In 1769, he travelled to France, and returning to Germany, met Lessing in Hamburg, and became court preacher to Count Schaumburg-

Lippe. In 1774 he published *Another Philosophy of History*, which combatted cosmopolitanism and rationalism. In 1776, he left for Weimar where he met Goethe, and published on Hebrew poetry, and his *Ideas on the Philosophy of Human History* (1784–91). Some of these ideas were reconsidered, under the impact of the French Revolution, in his 1793 *Letters on the Progress of Humanity*.

8 Holbach, Paul-Henri Thiry, Baron d' (1723–89), was of Swiss origin, and made a fortune as a financier in Paris. He gathered round him a group which included d'Alembert, Diderot, Buffon, Raynal and Rousseau. He attacked organised religion and argued for the sole reality of the material world. Much of his work was clandestinely published to avoid censorship, but he also wrote articles for the *Encyclopédie* on religion and on earth sciences. His 1770 *Système de la Nature* was his most famous work, and was attacked by Voltaire and by Frederick II of Prussia.

9 Kant, Immanuel (1724–1804), came from a strongly Pietist background in Prussia. After studying at the University at Königsburg, he became professor of mathematics and philosophy there in 1756. Kant was influenced by d'Alembert and by Rousseau, as well as by the Scots philosopher David Hume. His most famous work, the *Critique of Pure Reason* appeared in 1783. In 1784 he took part in a prize competition to answer the question 'What is Enlightenment?', and in 1795, published a *Project for Perpetual Peace*. Though Kant's reflections on the basis of rationality proceeded from Locke's rejection of innate ideas, he asked whether reason or the soul could be autonomous or independent of sense impressions.

10 La Mettrie, Julien Offroy de (1709–51), was born in Caen, and educated by Jesuits. He studied medicine at Leiden, where he was a student of Boerhave. These medical interests led him to a materialist position affirmed in his 1747 *L'Homme Machine* (*Man the Machine*) and the 1748 *Discourse on Happiness*. La Mettrie was much influenced by Epicurian philosophy of which he published an analysis in 1750. These views attracted hostility from Catholics and Protestants alike, and La Mettrie was forced to leave Leiden for Berlin, where he was welcomed by Frederick II. Nor was much *philosophe* opinion in his favour, as his thinking ran counter to much optimism, and to the idea that morality was somehow 'natural' and therefore innate.

11 Locke, John (1637–1704), author of the *Essay Concerning Human Understanding* (1690), and one of the key figures of the early Enlightenment. This work was of fundamental importance because it criticised Descartes' doctrine of innate ideas, and thus opened the way for much subsequent thinking by Hume, Condillac, Kant and others, on the meaning of human intelligence. Locke was also seen as a pioneer of the struggle for religious tolerance, after his 1689 *Letters on Toleration*, as well as his *The Reasonableness of Christianity* of 1695. Locke's influence on Voltaire was very strong, as it was on Rousseau, whose *Emile ou de l'éducation* (1762) was affected by his 1693 *Thoughts Concerning Education*. The Enlightenment also gained from Locke's *Second Treatise on Civil Government* the basis of its thinking on the idea of the contractual nature of society and government.

12 **Mendelssohn**, Moses (1729–86), grand-father of the composer, was the first major Jewish figure to intervene in the Enlightenment. He profited by the climate of religious toleration enforced by Frederick II to form an intellectual circle and publish widely, while at the same time composing in Hebrew, including a valuable commentary on Maimonides. Mendelssohn contributed to contemporary debates on religious toleration and Jewish emancipation, though insisting on the necessity for cultural diversity and avoiding uniformity. He contributed to the 1784 debate on the definition of 'Enlightenment', and wrote widely on aesthetics. Mendelssohn's work demonstrates the capacity of Enlightenment debates to mobilise thinkers right across ethnic and religious lines.

13 **Montesquieu**, Charles-Louis de Secondat, Baron de la Brède et de (1689–1755), was a member of a prominent family among the legal nobility of France, and he himself was President of the *Parlement* or sovereign appeal court of Bordeaux from 1726. The year 1721 saw the appearance of his first major work, the *Persian Letters*, a satire on the institutions of France, as well as presenting a less idealised view of the Orient than was the usual. *The Spirit of the Laws* (*Esprit des Lois*) (1748) was equally a best-seller widely translated, and one of the most widely diffused works of the Enlightenment, especially after it attracted the hostility of the church and was placed on the Index in 1751. Montesquieu argues for the inevitability of different systems of government, because of the way in which states are moulded by climate, geography, history, extent and by the '*morale*' of inhabitants.

14 **Newton**, Isaac (1642–1727), has often been seen as the founder of modern cosmology, after his theory of universal attraction, or gravitation, was set forward in his *Philosophiae Naturalis Principia Mathematica* (1687). Newton, who was a Fellow of Trinity College, Cambridge and Master of the Royal Mint, pursued fundamental research in optics, and was often seen, especially in Europe, as an exemplar of empirical, rationalist research. However, Newton also worked on alchemical problems and on numerical interpretations of Biblical prophecy.

15 **Quesnay**, François (1694–1774). After an eventful early life, Quesnay became a surgeon employed first by the Duc de Villeroi, then by Louis XV. His quarters at Versailles became a meeting place for Diderot, Turgot and Mirabeau. He is most associated with the new economic theory called Physiocracy which was discussed in Quesnay's articles for the *Encyclopédie*. Physiocracy sees land as the sole source of wealth, and advocates strong monarchy to guarantee the operation of a free market, in land and agricultural products. Quesnay's major works were his *Droit naturel* of 1765 and his *Maximes générales du government économique d'un royaume agricole* of the same year. His theories also influenced Karl Marx.

16 **Raynal**, Guillaume-Thomas, Abbé (1713–96), was a priest in minor orders who until 1750 earnt a living tutoring and through journalism. The publication of his *Anecdotes littéraires* in 1750 secured Raynal a rising place among Paris intelligentsia. In 1770 he produced the work on which his modern reputation rests, the *Histoire philosophique et politique des établissements et du commerce des Européens dans les deux Indes*, one of the first major histories of European

colonialism, a vast compendium of geographical and economic knowledge, as well as an argument for the morality of commerce, and the immorality of slavery. This book, produced with the help of Diderot, produced such fame for Raynal, that he left Paris for the provinces to try to reduce the inconvenience of publicity. He was an opponent of the French Revolution.

17 Rousseau, Jean-Jacques (1712–78), was born in Geneva, where he was raised by his father, a watchmaker. Leaving Geneva, he entered a vagabond existence, converted to Catholicism in Turin, and became linked to Mme de Warens at Chambéry from 1736 to 1738. Focussed at this period on music, he arrived in Paris in 1742, and became friendly with Diderot. The 1740s saw him moving increasingly to writing, beginning with articles for the *Encyclopédie*. In 1750, Rousseau's *Discours sur les sciences et les arts* won a prize competition at the Academy of Dijon, which was followed in 1755 by the *Discours sur l'origine de l'inegalité parmi les hommes*. Disputes with Voltaire and Diderot followed. Other major works were his novel *Julie ou la Nouvelle Héloïse* (1761); *Emile ou de l'éducation* and *Du Contrat Social* (1762). His autobiography the *Confessions* appeared posthumously between 1782 and 1788. His influence, particularly that of the *Social Contract*, actually increased during the French Revolution.

18 Turgot, Anne-Robert-Jacques (1727–81), began his career as an officeholder in the Paris Parlement and collaborated on the *Encyclopédie*, with articles mainly on economics. He became *Intendant*, or royal civil governor of the province of the Limousin in 1761, and Finance Minister from 1774–76. One of the few Enlightenment thinkers to have held high office in France, his economic ideas closely resembled those of the Physiocrats such as Quesnay, though he was also influenced by Adam Smith. His career in government was undermined by his support for a free market in wheat, which led to high prices, and riots all over the Isle de France, the *Guerre des Farines*, in 1775. He was also opposed to the existence of the artisan guilds, which he saw as a restriction on free trade.

19 Voltaire, François-Marie Arouet, dit (1694–1778), was one of the dominant figures of the Enlightenment, due to his longevity, his enormous output, his capacity to mobilise public opinion, and his relations with the great. Born into a legal family and educated by Jesuits, he was quickly introduced at court and began his literary career as a dramatist, and made an important stay in England (1726–29), turning to history with his *Charles XII* (1731) and to political comment with the *Lettres anglaises* (1734). The favour of Mme de Pompadour made him court historian, and he was invited to Berlin by Frederick II in 1750–3. He used his prestige to save the lives and reputations of the Calas and Sirvin families, and produced in 1763 his *Treatise on Toleration*.

Suggestions for further reading

In keeping with the approach towards the Enlightenment adopted in this account, these pointers towards deeper analysis proceed thematically, rather than being geared to specific chapters.

1 General surveys. The Enlightenment, however defined (chapter 1) has been treated in a large number of general works. Besides those mentioned in the text, the reader might consult examples of an older interpretative style, well represented by the lively writing of P. Hazard, *The European Mind 1680–1715* (first published in French, 1935, English translation, Cleveland: Meridian, 1963); and *European Thought in the Eighteenth-Century: From Montesquieu to Lessing* (1946, Cleveland: Meridian, 1963). Norman Hampson, *The Enlightenment* (Harmondsworth: Penguin Books, 1968) is valuable for its extended treatment of science as a major component of the Enlightenment, especially in relation to religion and history. Franco Venturi's perception of the importance of the European 'fringes' is at work in E. Bene and I. Kovacs (eds.), *Les Lumières en Hongrie, en Europe centrale et en Europe Orientale* (Budapest, 1975). The Enlightenment problem of founding an ethical system on 'nature' is addressed in Lester G. Crocker, *Nature and Culture: Ethical Thought in the French Enlightenment* (Baltimore: Johns Hopkins University Press, 1963). From a very different viewpoint, Lucien Goldmann, *The Philosophy of the Enlightenment: The Christian Burgess and the Enlightenment* (Cambridge, MA: Harvard University Press, 1973) examines ambiguities of the Enlightenment from a Marxist perspective. Even more controversial is the work of Margaret C. Jacob, *The Radical Enlightenment: Pantheists, Freemasons and Republicans* (London: George Allen and Unwin, 1981), which attempts to argue for a much more radical character to Enlightenment thought. Its conclusions should be compared to the approach adopted in the present volume, which argues fairly consistently for a view of the Enlightenment as paralysed by its own social, political, and intellectual contradictions in its attempts to change the world. The student must decide for him or herself which of these seems more convincing. Jacob's work should also be compared with Ira O. Wade, *The Intellectual Origins of the French Enlightenment* (Princeton, NJ: Princeton University Press, 1971), which also addresses the problem of early Enlightenment radicalism.

There is a limited number of comprehensive anthologies of Enlightenment writing. S. Eliot and Beverley Stern (eds.), *The Age of Enlightenment* (2 vols., New York: Barnes and Noble, 1979) is extremely full, but fails to give any space to Rousseau. Peter Gay, *The Enlightenment* (New York: Simon and Schuster, 1973) is almost equally full though paying less attention to science and the arts, and more to political writing. Jane Rendall (ed.), *The Origins of the Scottish Enlightenment 1707–76* (London, 1978) is the unique anthology on this topic.

Writings on individual thinkers are legion. The following is only a selection, and the list could easily be multiplied tenfold. Many 'minor' figures, on the other hand, still await modern, or indeed any, biographical treatment. John Locke is well served by John Yolton's *John Locke and the Way of Ideas* (New York: Oxford University Press, 1956). The best short biography of Voltaire is H.T. Mason, *Voltaire, A Biography* (Baltimore: Johns Hopkins University Press, 1981), which should be supplemented by J.H. Brumfitt, *Voltaire, Historian* (Oxford: Oxford University Press, 1958) and I.O. Wade, *The Intellectual Development of Voltaire* (Princeton: Princeton University Press, 1970). The literature on Rousseau is huge. Maurice Cranston, *Jean-Jacques: the Early Life and Work of Jean-Jacques Rousseau* (London: Allen Lane, 1983) is a good introduction, while not superseding Ronald Grimsley, *The Philosophy of Rousseau* (Oxford: Oxford University Press, 1973). J.L. Talmon's controversial *The Rise of Totalitarian Democracy* (London: Secker and Warburg, 1952) deeply marked by reflection on the Holocaust, argues that Rousseau's idea of the General Will prefigured much of twentieth-century totalitarian ideology. This should be supplemented by J. Derathé, *Jean-Jacques Rousseau et la science politique de son temps* (Paris: Armand Colin, 1950). Newton has been subjected to increasing examination in recent times, especially since the publication of the corpus of Newton's manuscripts by Richard Westfall, whose *Never at Rest: A Biography of Isaac Newton* (Cambridge University Press, 1980), should be supplemented by Betty Jo Teeter Dobbs, *The Foundations of Newton's Alchemy: or the 'hunting of the green lyon'* (Cambridge University Press, 1975); Henry Guerlac, *Newton on the Continent* (Ithaca, NY: Cornell University Press, 1981); M.C. Jacob, *The Newtonians and the English Revolution, 1689–1720* (Hassocks, Sussex: Harvester Press, 1976); I.B. Cohen, *Franklin and Newton* (Philadelphia: American Philosophical Society, 1956). On Montesquieu, the classic biography is R. Shackleton, *Montesquieu: A Critical Biography* (Oxford: Oxford University Press, 1960). The older study by E. Carcasonne, *Montesquieu et le problème de la constitution française au XVIIIe siècle* (Paris, 1926) explores his input into a key area of political debate in the conflict over the powers of absolutism in the Enlightenment. The co-editors of the *Encyclopédie* have always attracted much attention. Ronald Grimsley, *Jean d'Alembert 1717–83* (Oxford: Clarendon Press, 1963) is still useful, and should be read with Arthur Wilson, *Diderot: The Testing Years 1713–1759* (New York: Oxford University Press, 1969). David Hume is most accessibly reached in E.C. Mossner, *The Life of David Hume*, 2nd edn (Oxford: Clarendon Press, 1980). Kant can be approached via Stefan Körner's readable *Kant* (London: Penguin, 1955). Herder and Vico are compared in E. Callot, *Les trois moments de la philosophie théologique de l'histoire: Vico, Herder, Hegel* (Paris: Vrin, 1974) and in F.M. Barnard, *Herder's Social and Political Thought* (Oxford: Oxford University Press, 1965). For d'Holbach, A.C. Kors, *D'Holbach's Circle: An Enlightenment in Paris* (Princeton: Princeton University Press, 1977) also shows the group activity which supported the radical atheist; radical opinions are also explored in D.W. Smith, *Helvétius: A Study of Persecution* (Oxford: Clarendon Press, 1965).

Conflicts over the meaning of Enlightenment may be further explored in E.

Behr, 'In Defense of Enlightenment: Foucault and Habermas', *German Studies Review*, 2 (1988), 97–109 and in Jürgen Habermas, *Der Philosophische Diskurs der Moderne: Zwölf Vorlesungen* (Frankfurt-am-Main: Suhrkamp, 1985). General historical background to the eighteenth century can be explored in W. Doyle, *The Old European Order, 1660–1800* (Oxford: Oxford University Press, 1981), still probably the fullest survey. On religious history, whose themes run so strongly through the Enlightenment, G. Craig, *The Church in the Age of Reason* (Oxford, 1960) is a reliable survey. Religious conflict within the Catholic church, and its considerable political consequences, are studied in Dale Van Kley, *The Jansenists and the Expulsion of the Jesuits from France 1757–1765* (New Haven, 1975), while C. Becker, *The Heavenly City of the Eighteenth-Century Philosophers* (New Haven: Yale University Press, 1932) points out that the anti-religious positions taken by some leading thinkers succeeded only in erecting an alternative religion of 'reason'. Robert Mauzi, *L'idée de bonheur dans la littérature et la pensée française au XVIIIè siècle* (Paris: Colin, 1960), explores one of the major ideas replacing traditional religious thinking about man's place on earth. Henry F. May, *The Enlightenment in America* (New York: Oxford University Press, 1976), similarly stresses the role of religion, although it should be compared with the classic account by Frank Manuel, *The Eighteenth Century Confronts the Gods* (New York, 1967), which shows other strands of the Enlightenment concerned with the demystification of religion. G.R. Cragg, *Reason and Authority in Eighteenth-Century England* (Cambridge, 1964), and Hans Frei, *The Eclipse of Biblical Narrative* (New Haven, 1977), tell different aspects of the same story of the impact of comparative religion on the status of Christianity. On the science of the Enlightenment, still so entangled with theology, there is no overall survey. Jacques Roger, *Buffon: un philosophe au Jardin du Roi* (Paris, 1992) is the fruit of a life-time's erudition, as is his *Les sciences de la vie dans la pensée française au XVIIIè siècle* (Paris, 1963). D.G. Charlton, *New Images of the Natural* (Cambridge, 1984) and C. Glacken, *Traces on the Rhodian Shore: Nature and Culture in Western Thought* (Berkeley, 1967) each explore aspects of the central Enlightenment metaphor of 'nature'. K.M. Baker, *Condorcet: From Natural Philosophy to Social Mathematics* (Chicago, 1975) discusses the increasing interaction between the developing social sciences of the late Enlightenment, and the physical and mathematical sciences. The impact of science on the understanding of the history of the globe, is examined in P. Rossi, *The Dark Abyss of Time: The History of the Earth and the History of Nations from Hooke to Vico* (Chicago, 1984). While the impact of science on views of gender was very great, much older thinking also played a part, as shown by George Rousseau and Roy Porter (eds.), *Sexual Underworlds of the Enlightenment*. Women's own contribution to science is examined in Londa Schiebinger, *The Mind has no Sex? Women in the Origins of Modern Science* (Cambridge, MA, 1989). The relevance of the *philosophe* role to women are examined in Katherine Clinton, 'Femme et philosophe: Enlightenment Origins of Feminism', *Eighteenth-Century Studies*, 8 (1975), 283–99. The non-European world was also seen, as were women, as somehow 'natural'. Aspects of this connection are explored in the work of Raynal's collaborator, in Yves Bénot, *Diderot: De l'athéisme à l'anti-colonialisme* (Paris, 1970), and in Gilbert Chinard (ed.), Introduction to *Supplément au Voyage de Bougainville* (Paris, 1933). It was on the economies of the colonial world that much of the economic systems of the Enlightenment depended, as well as the power of many states. Aspects of these issues are addressed in Richard Herr, *The Eighteenth-Century Revolution in Spain* (Princeton, NJ, 1958); I. Hont and M. Ignatieff (eds.), *Wealth and Virtue. The Shaping of Political Economy in the Scottish Enlightenment* (Cambridge, 1983) shows the formation of some key economic ideas. L. Krieger, *Kings and Philosophers 1689–1789* (New York, 1970) examines the ambiguous relations between monarchs and leading thinkers, while Ronald Meek (ed.), *The Economics of Physiocracy* (Cambridge, MA, 1962), looks at the formation of another important set of economic theory. Ernst Wangermann, *The Austrian Achievement 1700–1800* (New York, 1973) looks at the stormy life of Enlightenment policies under Joseph II and Maria Theresa, as does Derek Beales, *Joseph II: in the Shadow of Maria Theresa, 1741–1780* (Cambridge, 1987). See also the classic study by S.L. Kaplan, *Bread, Politics and Political Economy in the Reign of Louis XV* (2 vols., The Hague, 1976). See also, on economic arguments, A.O. Hirschman, *The Passions and the Interests: Political Arguments for Capitalism before its Triumph* (Princeton, NJ, 1977).

Index